BERKSHIRE AND THE VALE OF WHITE HORSE

Roger Higham

BERKSHIRE
and the Vale of White Horse

B. T. Batsford Ltd
London

First published 1977

Photoset by Weatherby Woolnough, Wellingborough, Northants
Printed by J. W. Arrowsmith Ltd, Bristol
for the publishers B. T. Batsford Ltd
4 Fitzhardinge Street, London W1H 0AH
ISBN 7134 0681 X

Contents

Acknowledgements

The author and publishers would like to thank the following for their permission to reproduce the photographs which appear in this book: A. F. Kersting, F.R.P.S., nos 3, 4, 6, 7, 8, 11, 12, 14, 15, 16, 17, 18, 19; Raymond Lea, nos 1, 2, 5, 9, 10, 20, 21; Kenneth Scowen, F.I.I.P., F.R.P.S., nos 13, 22, 23. The map is by Patrick Leeson

Illustrations

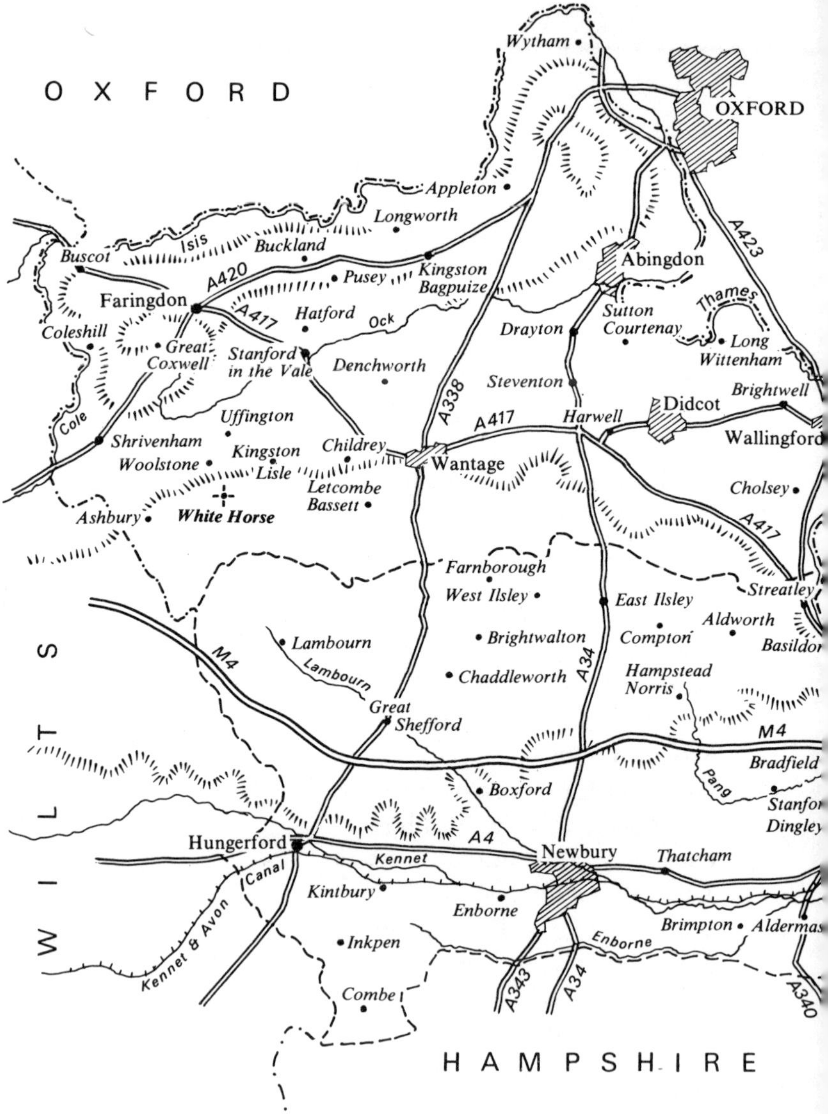

OXFORD
OXFORD
Wytham
Appleton
Longworth
Isis
Buckland
Buscot
A420
Pusey
Kingston Bagpuize
Abingdon
A423
Thames
Faringdon
A417
Hatford
Ock
Sutton Courtenay
Drayton
Long Wittenham
Coleshill
Great Coxwell
Stanford in the Vale
Denchworth
Steventon
Brightwell
A338
Didcot
Cole
Uffington
A417
Harwell
Wallingford
Shrivenham
Kingston Lisle
Childrey
Wantage
Woolstone
Letcombe Bassett
Cholsey
Ashbury
White Horse
A417
Farnborough
West Isley
East Ilsley
Streatley
Aldworth
Compton
Lambourn
Brightwalton
Basildon
M4
Lambourn
Chaddleworth
A34
Hampstead Norris
Great Shefford
M4
Bradfield
Pang
Boxford
WILTS
Hungerford
A4
Newbury
Thatcham
Kennet
Canal
Kintbury
Enborne
Brimpton
Kennet & Avon
Inkpen
Enborne
A343
A34
A340
Combe
HAMPSHIRE

BERKSHIRE
and the Vale of White Horse

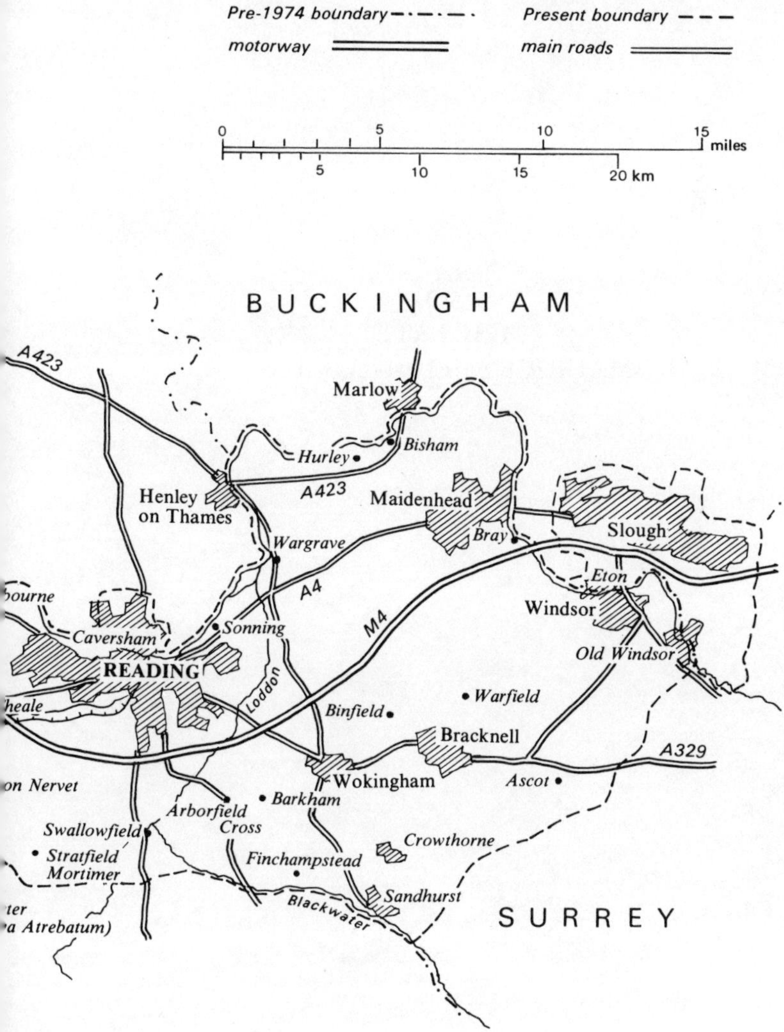

TO
THE LATE
MAURICE SNELLING, C.B.E.

Introduction

There is a huge quantity of literature about the counties of Kent, Sussex, Hampshire, Devonshire and most of the other southern regions of England: there is a comparative famine of information available concerning Berkshire. Why?

Berkshire has scenery as varied as any, from river meadow to forest and from fertile farmland to windswept Downs; there are villages which can scarcely be rivalled anywhere for the picturesque qualities alleged to be inherent in old timber and thatched roofs or in weathered and mellowed stone; its historical connections, from the remarkable preponderance of Iron Age hill-forts to its central and vital part in the struggle between king and parliament, could fill several books, and its seat of kings, the very root and core of English historical tradition, has already done so.

But apart from Windsor, what are the 'tourist attractions'? What other castles? Wallingford, which is hardly there at all? No cathedrals; no moving and awe-inspiring monastic monuments; no splendid, extravagant, baroque palaces; no mountains; no deep ravines with roaring, dashing torrents; no great lakes; no windy cliffs; no smooth white sands – no sea-side at all!

No 'tourist attractions', no guide-books: no wonder. But no grief, either, for Berkshire's beauties and fascinations are of a more subtle kind, which those who have no eyes to see, cannot see. 'Blind, blind, blind!' as Betsy Trotwood said to poor half-cooked Copperfield. Who needs stone walls and towers who can see the mighty earthen walls of Walbury and share with its starved, scared garrisons the long apprehensive scrutiny of the wide panorama, the distant hills and the threatening wilderness; why pine for cathedrals when faith speaks from the simplicity of parish churches, sites used and re-used, over and over again, materials mended, doorways and windows, if serviceable, always retained until past repair and another renewal unavoidable. What palaces in their empty grandeur can speak half as much of the men and women who have lived in them as old manor-houses, standing as immemorially, near to their proprietary churches, enlarged and altered but always bearing the imprint of humanity?

A landscape without men is a fine and inspiring sight: but a landscape made by men, to which each generation, in its turn, has contributed some slight change, is worth profound study, because it speaks of the nation's history; and a nation's history is its memory, and a nation with a memory as long as England's does not need to fall back on mendacious myths.

Berkshire's history, with its boundaries, has been disrupted. In 1974 the counties of England and Wales suffered one of their periodic spring-cleaning bouts, when the Civil Service housemaids tidied up some of the remaining anomalies (and created some more) in the interests of administrative convenience. Berkshire, as a result of this decree, had to give more than a third of its total area to Oxfordshire. The boundary, which used simply to run along the little River Cole to the Upper Thames or Isis, then along that river without any further ado the whole way to Runnymede, now traces a course about as straightforward, by comparison, as that of a deranged earwig, along the top of the Downs from somewhere near Lambourn to somewhere near Streatley. How, I wondered, did the inhabitants of northern Berkshire appreciate finding themselves suddenly in Oxfordshire after so many centuries' experience of Berkshire? The answer as I should have known, seems to be that they have not lived through all those centuries, just their own lifetime, and their personal experience of Berkshire all too often had been that Reading, the county town, seemed remote from them and it took a long time to persuade it to get anything done. As the Vale of White Horse District, with administrative offices in Abingdon, they feel a new spirit, almost as if they were in a little county of their own.

But this book is about Berkshire, historical Berkshire, and a division made in its territory as recently as 1974 must be ignored if the book is to treat its subject honestly: would a German, writing the history of his country, leave out its eastern half?

The county's name is unique, in that it is the only one of the southern counties to be named after a natural element rather than from either a tribal name (Dorset, Somerset, Sussex) or an old area-name (Kent, Surrey) or after its principal town (Hampshire, Oxfordshire). Asser, a Welsh monk who wrote a biography of King Alfred the Great during the latter's lifetime referred to 'the district called Bearrocscire which district is so-called from the Berroc wood where the box-tree grows most abundantly'. Very probably he was right, but where did the Berroc wood get its name from? The spelling Bearroc helps, because there was a British word 'barro' (Welsh 'bar') meaning top, summit, so, as Professor Ekwall concludes, 'the forest was no doubt named from a hill "B(e)arroc"!'

This place-name derivation also provides evidence of the extremely careful path one has to tread in the matter of invasions, and ethnic distinctions. There were several waves of newcomers to south-east Britain from the middle Bronze Age to the late Iron Age, and they did not remain independent of one another. The last arrivals, the Belgic Atrebates, came because the great Gallic revolt against the Romans had failed and life was altogether too hot for them in Gaul. They formed a warrior aristocracy over the incumbent Celtic tribes, under their chieftain or king Commius, minted coins and seem to have been remarkably well organised, with their capital at Calleva. Their territory covered most of Berkshire's present area and stretched southward into Hampshire, and their dynasty lasted until the Berkshire part was annexed by the invasion from across the Thames of the Catuvellauni under their king Cunobelin (about whom Shakespeare, using the name Cymbeline, wrote a play) in about 25 A.D. Twenty years later the Romans had arrived and the area had become a part of the province, with Calleva, now called Calleva Atrebatum, as its tribal capital.

The Atrebates had mingled with the people over whom they ruled, and the Romans inter-married with all the Britons, who, civilised to a higher degree than ever before or for many centuries after, could be called Romano-British. The influx of the Germanic Saxons, following the abandonment by the Roman government of Britannia as a province (by that time it actually comprised five provinces), into the southern regions was a slow process: periods of fighting were interspersed with periods of settling down with the Romano-Britons. Persistent outbreaks of pestilence devastated towns and caused the incoming Saxons to avoid them. Calleva survived until some time in the 6th century when either a fresh wave of Saxon hostility or another plague finished off the inhabitants.

So it happens that, in Berkshire as in other parts of England, there are names which have been adopted by each wave of settlers in turn. The majority of place-names in Berkshire have a Saxon origin, but the river-names, and the county's name itself, are Celtic.

The characteristic geological feature of Berkshire is chalk: a bed of rock 700 feet thick dips gently southwards, with its exposed northern edge forming a ridge, running eastward from Ashbury to Streatley, on the Thames. The chalk bed passes south under the Kennet valley, and turns up sharply again to the surface to form the high scarp face of the North Hampshire Downs at Inkpen Hill. The chalk extends as a bedrock into East Berkshire: the low hills by Sonning and Remenham and Cookham are chalk, and so is the outlying hump on which Windsor Castle stands. But this eastern region is not characteristic chalkland, like the Downs; it has been weathered away and covered with a deposit called clay-with-flints, on which good crops and woods can grow.

The Vale of White Horse and the Upper Thames valley are based on clay formations, much covered by sands and gravels deposited by the river systems, and between them runs the North Berkshire Ridge, from Coleshill to Wytham, which consists of an outcrop of limestone and sandstone, in parts called Corallic because they contain masses of fossil corals: these stones are used for building and since they can be flaked successfully, roofs are slated with them too.

South and east of the Kennet valley, the soils are mainly stiff clays and pebbly sands; the Bagshot beds are those which support the characteristic heathland and pine forest of the Berkshire and Hampshire borders, the region of Sandhurst, Camberley, rifle-ranges and training areas.

Stone on the Ridge and in the Vale of White Horse, chalk, surprisingly enough, on the north scarp of the Downs, flints everywhere, and above all timber from the abundant woods and brick, from the eminently suitable clays, are the principal building materials. Brick-making has gone on in Berkshire for longer than in most places, at least since the fourteenth century, so the most frequently encountered form of domestic house or cottage in Berkshire is timber-framed, with an in-filling of brick, and a roof either tiled or thatched. This kind of house has blended so well with the landscape that it gives the impression of having grown in it naturally, a soft interplay with plant growth that gives subtle expression to man's long acquaintance with soil and the weather; Berkshire villages are the leading attractions of the County, because they are essential clues to the mystery of that which constitutes civilization.

The feature of Berkshire that has done more than any other to form the County's historical character is its position as a thoroughfare. It can claim no river except the Ock as entirely its own; the others flow through it to the greatest, the Thames. Important roads, the Bath road, the Oxford road through the gap in the Downs made by the Thames, and now the great M4 motorway, run through it; old battles for possession of these routes are prominent in Berkshire history. The Kennet and Avon Canal, and the main lines of the Great Western Railway have not been fought for, but they have had no less profound an influence on the formation of towns and the livelihood of their inhabitants. It is no coincidence that the chapter divisions of this book are based so overwhelmingly on the County's thoroughfares: rivers, roads, railways form the limits to each, because they have all brought their own particular features and affected the subsequent development of each area in their own way.

I have explored Berkshire mainly on foot, about 450 miles of it, in order better to see, feel, smell and touch it; I have begun the book in the extreme northern section near Oxford, and finished in the extreme eastern, near Windsor, and in between I have visited as many of the towns and villages as possible. There are some, too many in fact, that pressure of time has deprived me of the chance of seeing: that does not mean they are not worth visiting. There is something of interest to see, for those who know where to look, in all places.

ONE

North Wessex

Before the revision of county boundaries in 1974, the unique character of Berkshire's was that no other county could claim a bank of the River Thames along the whole of one of its sides. Beginning at St John's Bridge, near Buscot, the river constituted Berkshire's northern boundary all the long way to Runnymede. In this sense, the Thames seemed to be almost Berkshire property, if the ancient claim of riparian rights counted for anything. The new, shrunken Berkshire has lost that claim, its share of the river almost halved; the remaining half might be the wider, more useful and more important reaches, yet the upper stretch, now entirely in Oxfordshire, included the lovelier, wilder, less thronged parts.

Thomas Hardy has supplied the title for this first chapter: he applied it to the whole of old Berkshire, but it will serve equally well for the Vale of White Horse District which, newly constituted as a part of Oxfordshire, is almost a county in its own right; and of that district, what better title to describe the most northerly region of it, that area which is really a peninsula of land, caught in a colossal meander of the great river? To travel from Newbridge to Abingdon by road is a simple matter of eight or nine miles: to repeat the journey by the river is nearer to twenty-five. Using the road, the A415, as the southern boundary, then, I shall try to describe this tongue of land with the past events and people associated with it.

The country is for the most part hilly, rising from the plains of the valley of the little River Ock northward to the wooded heights of Hurst Hill and Wytham Hill, over 500 feet above sea level. To

1 The Town Hall, Abingdon

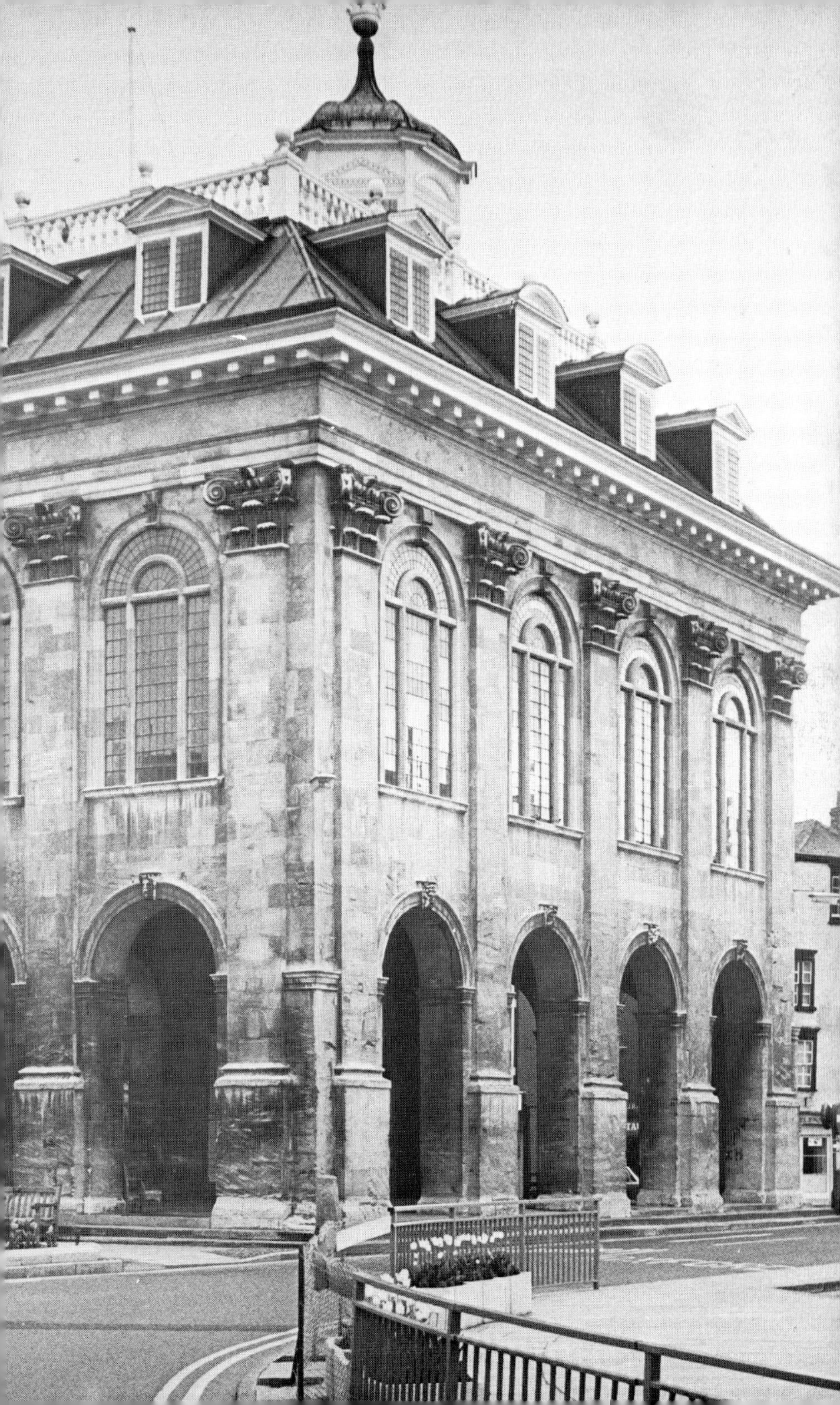

BELL HOTEL
MARKET PLACE
BARCLAYS

mountain folk, talk of 'heights' of such dimensions may seem a tale told by an idiot, but southern England is not mountainous, its charms are of a different order, and the terms used are comparative. I shall begin this tour of Berkshire and its lost province, the Vale of White Horse, on the banks of the shallow Ock where the Romans forded it. Close to the river the Celts of the Iron Age had a settlement and a little circular religious shrine: rivers were usually credited by them with a guiding or protective spirit and it was probably natural to offer the river-god some kind of homage. The shrine was rebuilt in Roman times, and then a proper temple in the form of a square: Roman administrative government seldom had any objection to local deities. The site is distinguished now by a substantial stone-built inn, painted pink, called 'Noah's Ark'.

A field-track cuts off the corner between this Roman road, now the A338, and my southern boundary for this chapter, the A415 road, and meets it near Marcham. Away south on the river marshes is Marcham Mill, which has certainly existed in some form for a very long time, since it once belonged to the Abbey of Abingdon, until (it is said) a grateful epicurean abbot gave it away to his cook. Marcham, in common with most of the villages of both the Vale of White Horse and the North Berkshire Ridge which lie between Ock and Thames, is built mainly of stone; the ridge is an outcrop of mid-Jurassic limestones and sandstones, called Corallic because some of the limestones contain masses of fossil corals. It was quarried to build the Oxford colleges, and it has contributed toward the majority of the houses, churches, barns and cottages of both Ridge and Vale. The stone also flakes well so has been used for roofing slates too: one of the most attractive features of villages in this region is the combination in them of stone walls with a variety of stone slates, tiles or thatch in the roofs. Marcham is like that, the cottages and houses are of all ages from the sixteenth century to the twentieth: the house next to the churchyard, stone painted white, and stone-slated, is dated 1646 on a corner-stone. The church, like surprisingly many in Berkshire, was restored in the nineteenth century: there have been several outstanding periods of church building and rebuilding over the centuries, and the last century was one of them. Some of the results are the worst ever, but others are satisfactory; most are

2 Market Place, Faringdon

imitations of some other style, and the more disastrous are often combinations of two or three. All Saints, Marcham, was partially rebuilt in 1837, quite well, in Perpendicular style, and the tower and north chapel of the thirteenth century, with a triplet of lancets, were left intact. There are memorial brasses, also well restored, to Edmund and Margaret Fettiplace, with their coats of arms, dated 1560. The Fettiplaces, to be encountered later in this chapter at their manor-house at Appleton, were a family whose well-placed connections spread far and wide over the county.

Behind the church the grounds begin of Marcham Park, once the manor-house, but now Denman College, property of the National Federation of Women's Institutes: it is a nineteenth-century house but invisible from the road because entirely screened by its woods, and encircled by high stone walls.

The lane leading north from Marcham begins to climb up into the hilly ridge-country: not, as I have pointed out, exactly the Pennine Chain, but hilly compared with the level water-meadows of the Ock. From near a crossroads at the top a footpath snakes off between lines of concealing trees across the fields to Tubney Wood and the A338 road again, which shortly joins another Oxford-bound road, the A420, and the peace of the woodland footpath must be exchanged for the clamour of the highway, because an Oxford-bound road will have Oxford-bound traffic, and plenty of it. One of the advantages of travelling on foot is that one can generally avoid the battering of the senses attendant upon keeping company with main-road traffic, but occasionally there is no way round it, as when the road passes such a place as Besselsleigh.

There is more to be said about Besselsleigh than actually exists of it today: apart from a small hamlet half a mile further towards Oxford there is only the modern version of the manor-house, which is a school, and its chapel, which is the parish church; some explanation seems therefore needed.

There existed in 965 a settlement here called Leia, becoming Leie in Domesday Book; in 1412 the manor was held by one Petrus Besyles, whose family the sixteenth-century topographer John Leland knew by historical reputation to have been men 'of activity in feats of arms' who came 'out of Provence in France'. If this is the case, then a reasonable guess might be that they came to England first in the train of Henry III's Queen Eleanor of Provence when he married her in 1236, since a disturbing number (to English barons) of Provençal and Savoyard younger sons accompanied her in the hope of being rewarded with a few manors in the fertile and rich land of England. But this is only a guess. When the Besils became extinct the manor passed to the Fettiplaces, then in 1630 was bought from them by a rather egregious character called William Lenthall.

If Lenthall could be called a politician of his time, then he could be called a politician of any time, a sitter on the fence, a trimmer, a time-server, afraid of committing himself too deeply to any one side lest he spoil his chances should the other side prevail. Born in Henley-on-Thames in 1591, second son of a gentleman of Oxfordshire, he left Oxford without taking a degree, entered instead Lincoln's Inn and climbed rapidly to success in the Law. He represented Woodstock in the Short Parliament of April 1640 and in the Long Parliament, at the opening of which he was unanimously elected Speaker, and also appointed to the committee on the question of Ship-money. He was not, it seems, the best choice for Speaker, but was kept in the post because, although irritable, he was easy to appease and was complaisant. Clarendon says that he was 'a lawyer of good practice and no ill affections, but a very weak man and unequal to such a task'. The post of Speaker was an expensive one, and to compensate for this he was awarded other remunerative posts which, as sinecures, were always available for suitable recipients. Unfortunately, when the conflict with the King reached a head, all Lenthall's estates lay in the territory under the King's control, so he suffered considerably. In December 1644 a Royalist band captured his house at Besselsleigh, but shortly afterwards a party from the Parliamentary garrison of Abingdon recaptured it, and made sure that it would be of no further use to the Royalists by wrecking it.

Lenthall was still in the chair, reluctantly, during the progress of the bill to bring the King to trial, although he disapproved of the motion, and continued to occupy it after the King had been tried and executed, because he was afraid to admit his doubts. While feeling sympathy for the Royalists, he continued to serve Cromwell. Because he was afraid of showing his sympathies, he was reluctant to return to

London when Parliament was recalled, and because he was afraid of losing his possessions, allowed himself to be persuaded to return as Speaker. Cromwell, when he was Lord Protector, gave him a peerage, and he was afraid of losing it by offending Cromwell, yet kept in touch with the Royalists and had some hand in collusion with Monk to restore Charles II.

What this pusillanimous man did achieve to his lasting credit was to restore and repair the little church of St Lawrence in the grounds of his manor-house. It is a simple nave and chancel all in one with no division between, in stone with a stone-slated roof. It is of Norman origin, as shown by the south doorway, but was restored in the Perpendicular style in the fifteenth century. Lenthall's contribution, shortly after he had bought the manor, in 1632, was to restore and beautify the interior, and build (or rebuild) the bellcote. With the traffic flashing past on the adjacent road, the church seems rather forlorn, and is wisely kept locked. Roses grow about the lop-sided little porch, the bellcote is again being repaired; around one of the churchyard yews is an enclosure and the graves of some later Lenthalls of the eighteenth and nineteenth centuries.

A fifteenth-century Besils, Sir Peter, is said to have provided the stone from his manor to build a new bridge at Abingdon: by this time the prosperity of the town was evidently well-established, and attests to the affluence of its abbey. The town rose with the abbey: in Domesday Book no town is mentioned at all, only ten traders before the abbey gates. The story of its beginnings is a little complicated.

An abbey was founded in 675, but not on its present site: the first abbey was begun on the ridge at a place known as Boars Hill, north-east of Besselsleigh. This was the original Abingdon, a name derived from Aebbe's dun (Aebbe is a woman's name) but the monastery was destroyed by the Danes. In 955 it was refounded on its present site by St Aethelwold, brought by King Edred from Glastonbury to be its abbot. It reached the climax of its growth in the early twelfth century under Abbot Fabritius, whose influence increased the number of monks there from 28 to 78. Its wealth must have been at least conspicuous, however, by the fourteenth century still, judging by the following extract from Langland's *Piers Plowman*:

'Yet a king shall arise who shall purge all you men of Religion, and scourge you for the breaking of your Rule as Christ scourged the money-changers out of the Temple. And he shall reform all you nuns and monks and canons, and put you to your penance, till you return at last to your original Rule . . . .

'At that time the Abbot of Abingdon, and all his issue for ever, shall get such a blow from this king that nothing will cure it.'

But already by this time, the wool-trade had been well established and was becoming vitally important: by the time that a king did arise who smote the abbot and all his issue, and not only reformed the abbey but abolished it altogether, the wool-trade had become the town's principal sustenance.

Although clearly insubstantial at the time that the abbey was refounded on the site, there is evidence that it had been a centre of settlement of one sort or another from time immemorial: the latter phrase could with reason be used because the evidence shows signs of habitation in the Old and New Stone Ages, the Early and Middle Bronze Ages, the later Iron Age and some occupation during Britain's time as a Roman province. The site, the confluence of the Ock with the Thames with a firm bank for building on, suggests itself as a convenient place for settlement. Today, as the administrative centre of the new Vale of White Horse District Council, Abingdon has assumed the provincial importance of a minor county town; it has a large population (no doubt increased from 14,000 in 1961) and several industries to sustain it.

One administrative function which it no longer exercises is its prison, a great grey stone bastion, sited prominently by the river and bridge, built between 1805 and 1811, with a towering hexagonal centre block: the new District Council has imaginatively re-opened it as an Arts and Sports Centre. On the other side of the road a lane leads to the remaining Abbey buildings, near the river, the Long Gallery, a late fifteenth-century range in timber and stone, which originally had a timber gallery or cloister walk, and the Chequer, a square thirteenth-century block in stone. In the Market Square is a complex assortment of buildings: the central feature is the Abbey Gate, which has three archways, two of which are original to the fifteenth century, and attached to it is St Nicholas Church, which is not the Abbey church but a connected lay church, built probably in the late twelfth century, since it has a surviving late Norman doorway, but otherwise Perpendicular and restored in 1881; on the other, southern side of the gateway is a range of buildings which are difficult to sort out: they began life as the Hospitium of St John, a department of the Abbey for looking after travellers, were augmented and used as Roysse's Grammar School, with parts added and a storey raised on top in the 1730s, and are now used as municipal buildings. Behind the gateway are gardens where once stood the Abbey church: plenty of disorganised masonry lies about, and some has been piled into walls and arches, not very skilfully, to make fake ruins. The destruction of the once-great Abbey is therefore sadly comprehensive.

The building that really dominates the Market Place is the Town Hall, an immensely imposing and grandiose work built in 1678-1682 by Christopher Kempster, from a design that was the pattern for Sir Christopher Wren's Trinity College, Cambridge. These were just the years when the whole country, but especially London, was in a hysterical panic because of the perjurous disclosures of the execrable Titus Oates, and many good and innocent men had already been slaughtered, on his false evidence, because of their alleged complicity in the wholly fictitious 'Popish Plot'. At least something, in the shape of this fine Town Hall (the much-travelled Celia Fiennes called it the finest in England) of lasting value has emerged from that unsavoury era. The ground floor, partly supported by columns, was intended as a market-hall, the upper as Council Chambers. On top is a turret with an ogival cupola; there are here and there flourishes and touches of the Baroque.

South-west of it and close by the river is the big parish church of St Helen's, which was first reared, steeple and all, in the thirteenth century, but has been repaired and rebuilt since, notably in the fifteenth and sixteenth centuries in the fine Perpendicular style, and also in the nineteenth century. Its most remarkable possession is the roof-panel painting in the inner north aisle, of 1390, which Sir Nikolaus Pevsner says is unique in England; it shows the Tree of Jesse.

Some of the ordinary houses and shops of the town are well worth a study, because much survives even from the late Middle Ages. Buildings of stone do tend to remain for centuries where they were put, but one of the surprising features of Berkshire is the number of basically wooden houses, many of them thatched, which, uninsurable by normal actuarial standards because of the virtual racing certainty of destruction by fire at some time or another, have nevertheless managed to remain unconsumed for four or five hundred years. Stert Street has some of these: No. 3 is of the early sixteenth century, with a big overhanging jetty, Nos 31-38, a greengrocer and florist, with two gables, is from the fifteenth century. East St Helen's Street also has a couple of these aged timber houses. Some of them may have been in the process of building when the parish clerk of St Helen's made this entry in the Parish Register:

> '1569 – buried the 3 day of Marche, Margery Towsey, widdow, who was at the assize then holden, quit of witchecrafte layde to her charge, and dyed this day in the streete, sodenlie as she was going on her business.'

A road leads out north-eastward from Abingdon to the flat river-levels and the beginnings of the Ridge on which stands the village of Radley. As at Abingdon, this gently sloping land has been the chosen habitation place of people from the very earliest of times: finds of various sorts, burials, and grave-goods, have shown that people in the New Stone Age and all the stages of the Bronze Age found the site suitable for settlement. A stretch of grassy, bushy wasteland on the right of the road past the lane leading to Wick Hall, called Barrow Hills, gives a place-name indication of the site: the barrows are Bronze Age barrows. Also in the vicinity have been found signs of Iron Age, Roman and Saxon occupation (there is a Saxon barrow in the low-lying part of Radley, near the river). Often, hill-tops and river banks yield evidence of ancient occupation, the sites most suitable for people to inhabit when conditions were at their most primitive.

Radley Hall stands up on the Ridge and can be seen from the lower road. Built between 1721 and 1727 by Sir James Stonehouse, it is an impressive tall house of nine bays, in red brick with stone dressings, in a style reminiscent of Queen Anne but looking forward too to the graceful achievements of the later eighteenth century. When Sir George Bowyer, a nephew of the last Stonehouse, who had received a baronetcy for his services in the Navy under Lord Howe, bankrupted himself in the effort to find coal on his estate, he let the house for a Nonconformist school, which failed. In 1847 Dr William Sewell of the Oxford Movement took it for a new Church of England school; by the 1860s it had run up debts of some £40,000, but it was saved, expanded and firmly established, and it flourishes now as St Peter's College, Radley, with a very fine reputation, especially for boating.

The old church of Radley, St James's, stands by the lane near the drive to the school. It has a slender tower, is all in stone, and is another which had its origins in late Norman times: the stone font survives, with an arcading relief around it. There is a typically flamboyant memorial to an early seventeenth-century Stonehouse, and his wife and children, with its inscription all in Latin. The choir-stalls and misericords are also from the same period, and there is a huge canopy over the pulpit, in dark carved wood like the choir-stalls: it is much too big for the pulpit (which is in stone) and it is said that it comes from the Speaker's Chair in the House of Commons. Not unnaturally, one leaps to the conclusion that the wretched Lenthall had something to do with its removal, but there seems to be no suggestion of this by tradition. There is also, at the western end of the church, a twentieth-century contribution to its treasures in the form of a big embroidered pictorial map of the village, by members of its Women's Institute. North of the church there is a timber-framed house which looks as if it has lasted since the fifteenth century.

By the side of Radley Large Wood the road climbs into hillier, more thickly wooded country, passes over the Oxford road A34 by Sugworth Farm, across an earlier Oxford road and down into Sunningwell past another farm whose barns and outbuildings have all been cleverly converted to residences.

Sunningwell is a pretty village, in a valley, and consists mainly of stone cottages but there are also some which are timber-framed and brick. There is a duckpond opposite the church, which is a mainly Perpendicular building in stone, with a north tower, and has a wonderfully curious porch: it is seven-sided, in a combination of Perpendicular and Renaissance styles, with Ionic columns at the corners. It is supposed to have been given to the parish by Bishop John Jewel of Salisbury, who had been rector of Sunningwell in 1551. He was one of those Protestant clerics who spent the years of Queen Mary's reign abroad, and returned when she died: Elizabeth appointed him to his bishopric. Friar Roger Bacon is said to have conducted experiments with telescopes from the church tower, but if that is so it was certainly not this particular tower: he did it in the thirteenth century. Another clergyman with connections here was Dr Samuel Fell, Dean of Christ Church, Oxford, the father of the other Dr Fell about whom there is that unkind rhyme. Dr Samuel, not afraid to change his mind, unlike Speaker Lenthall was also not afraid to hold to his convictions despite the likely consequences. He was born in London in 1584, entered the church and at first was Calvinistic. Later he changed his opinions and actively assisted Archbishop William Laud, the butt of all the country's puritans, for which Laud gave him the deanery of Christ Church in 1638. His loyalty to Laud extended to loyalty to the King, and at the outbreak of the Civil War he was a conspicuous Royalist, which in Oxford was admittedly pretty safe. But in 1647 when he was re-appointed Vice-Chancellor, a panel of Parliamentary visitors came to Oxford, and Fell was summoned before them. He refused to go: he was imprisoned, and stripped of all his offices at the University. He retired to the rectory of Sunningwell (which in fact he had held since 1625) and lived there for two more years as a simple country parson. On 1 February 1649, when he heard of the execution of the King, he collapsed and died from the shock.

From Sunningwell a lane begins the climb up Foxcombe Hill, through the hamlet of Bayworth, where there used to be a manor-house belonging to the lords of Sunningwell, the Baskervilles, one of whom was a redoubtable military commander for Queen Elizabeth I, and another, Hannibal Baskerville, was several times indicted at Abingdon sessions for harbouring beggars: he is said to have given away nearly a third of his estate to the poor, including building a barn in which any wandering beggar could find shelter.

From Foxcombe Hill, which is near Boars Hill, the original site of Abingdon, there is a footpath which takes the visitor well away from the accumulation of out-of-town residences which has grown up in that area. This path leaves the hill-top houses and gardens behind and takes to the fields: in two miles the only habitation it passes as it climbs round the lower slopes of Hen Wood and Hurst Hill is a great stone farmhouse, newly tiled in ugly red, called Chilswell. There is a distant college of Oxford, it is true, on a hill above North Hinksey, but the folds of the hills and the ever-present foliage screen from view the suburban housing of outer Oxford. Instead, from 'the warm, green-muffled Cumnor hills', like Matthew Arnold's Scholar-Gipsy, 'the eye travels down to Oxford's towers'. Nothing intervenes to spoil the view, or the pastoral peace: it is in fact typical of this curious county of contrasts, that no matter how frantic the pace and clatter of the highways through it, at no more than a few minutes' remove from them all is quiet and serenity.

When the track descends from Hurst Hill it meets the Oxford road A338 and the few suburban-type streets of Chawley. Between Chawley and Cumnor there is a quarter of a mile of lane which is now cut in two by the works of a new motorway, being built, presumably, to by-pass all the other by-passes. This negotiated, there is the pleasant stone-built village of Cumnor, all up and down a hillside, with its church perched on a promontory. It is another late Norman church with additions and improvements of the three succeeding styles of the Middle Ages, a two-decker Jacobean pulpit in dark carved wood, a statue of Queen Elizabeth I in the vestry, and in the sanctuary a memorial tomb in grey stone, with brasses, to Anthony Forster, and a panegyric in Latin starting 'Anthony Forster, fine flower of his race. . . .' In the vestry, on the wall by the Queen's statue, are some pictures, letters and relics of the dramatic mystery of the death of Amy Dudley. This is the story used by Sir Walter Scott in *Kenilworth,* and it concerns the Queen, Robert Dudley, Earl of Leicester, and his wife Amy, and how rumour had it that the Earl, wishing to render himself eligible to marry the Queen, arranged to have his wife murdered while she was staying at Cumnor Place. She was found dead at the bottom of a flight of stairs there, and the important question was, and is, did she fall or was she pushed?

Robert Dudley and Amy Robsart were married in 1550, when they were both about 18; Dudley was often taken to court by his father, the Duke of Northumberland, but Amy stayed at home, a manor-house near Yarmouth granted to them by the Duke. Dudley, although involved in the tragic affair of Lady Jane Grey and sentenced to death, was released and pardoned in 1554 (Amy visited him while he was in the Tower). Elizabeth, on her accession, liked him: on 11 January 1559 she made him Master of Horse; on 23 April, Knight of the Garter and Privy Councillor; on 3 November he and Lord Hunsdon held the lists at Greenwich against all comers. The Queen granted him lands, licences and lieutenancies, and even contemplated marrying him (she was now 26) and in January 1560 the Spanish ambassador, de Quadra, described him as 'the king that is to be' and notes the indignation of people at his presumption.

Amy, Countess of Leicester, spent her time staying with friends in the country, most often with the Hydes at Denchworth, not far from Wantage, and during 1558 and 1559 Dudley often visited her there. Anthony Forster (of the memorial in Cumnor church), a personal friend of Dudley and also his steward, in charge of his private expenses, rented in 1560 Cumnor Place from its owner William Owen, and Amy moved there. Dudley spent most of his time at the Queen's court, while it was common gossip that he and the Queen would soon marry.

On Sunday 8 September 1560 the Countess suggested that the whole household should visit Abingdon Fair. The three ladies of the house, Mrs William Owen, Mrs Forster and a sister of Mr Hyde, stayed behind with Amy, but only Mrs Owen dined with her. Late in the day, the servants returned from Abingdon, and found Amy lying dead at the foot of the staircase in the hall. The other ladies said that she had been playing cards with them, had left the room, and must have fallen downstairs and broken her neck.

Dudley was with the Queen at Windsor when he heard the news; to his discredit he stayed there, merely directing a distant relative, Sir Thomas Blount, to go to Cumnor and organise a stringent enquiry. A key witness came forward: Mrs Pinto, Amy's maid. She said that she had heard Amy 'pray to God to deliver her from desperation'. Rumours were rampant, for example that Dudley had ordered Forster to throw her downstairs (never mind that Forster had not been there). On 13 September Dudley reiterated his insistance to Blount that a thorough and impartial investigation be arranged, and that all the jurors of the inquest be strangers to him. Their verdict was mischance or accidental death.

But the rumours were not scotched by the verdict: everyone assumed that Dudley had ordered his wife's murder. Did he not want her out of the way so that he could marry the Queen? It followed as night follows the day. But even Sir William Cecil, Secretary of the Queen's Council, who thoroughly disapproved of Dudley, came to the conclusion that there was really no evidence to support the rumours, that nothing could be proved against him. The whole sad episode did, of course, finish whatever chances Dudley might have had of becoming the Queen's consort. It is at least possible, on the maid's evidence, that it was suicide, although of all ways of ending one's life, falling downstairs seems to combine maximum discomfort with minimum chance of success. She could simply have fallen by accident.

Cumnor Place no longer exists: in 1811 the Earl of Abingdon pulled down the remaining ruins and, transporting them to Wytham, rebuilt the church there.

One at least of Cumnor's stone buildings, apart from the church, must have existed at the time of this drama: the inn, the Bear and Ragged Staff, appears from the front to be a product of the seventeenth century, but at the back, facing the courtyard, there is a surviving window in late Perpendicular style, with stone mullion and arched lights. Or was it filched from the ruins of Cumnor Place?

To reach Wytham from this direction is quite difficult: the very tip of this northerly peninsula is the mass of Wytham Hill and its lower slopes, and no road, no track, no public footpath crosses it. One must, by any means, tread circumspectly around it, for Wytham is on the far side, facing the river. The quickest way is to take to the A420, endure its tumult to Botley, find a way through the convolutions of the by-pass works, creep precariously along the side of the A34 which does not, as yet, offer an adequate footpath, and then slip away with a sigh of relief to a lane which follows a parallel course to the road, but higher up the hillside. This hillside, at a spot approximately mid-way between Botley and Wytham, is the site of a deserted village called

Seacourt: a branch stream of the Thames running parallel to the road is still called the Seacourt Stream. Wytham itself is another of those riverside sites beloved of ancient dwellers, evidence having been found there of successive settlements from the Early Bronze Age to Roman times, and the village existed by the same name at least as early as 957, when it appears as *Wihtham:* 'Ham (farmstead) by the bend', referring to the river's bend.

Wytham is a delightful village of stone cottages and houses, either thatched or stone-slated: even a new house in the village is built in precisely the same way, stone slates and all, and a big square dovecot in the yard of the tall old inn, the White Hart, shows that doves enjoy in Wytham the same provisions for shelter as humans. The entrance to the churchyard, next to the gates and lodge-house of Wytham Abbey, is a little doorway with a late Perpendicular arch which came from Cumnor Place and was re-used, and in fact the whole church, as mentioned, was rebuilt from Cumnor materials. An earlier Earl of Abingdon, the third, restored and replaced the brasses of Robert de Wightam and his wife Juliana, on an inscribed tombstone before the altar. Robert died in 1406 and is shown on the brass in the sort of armour that developed during the course of the Hundred Years War. The church also has a shiny new royal coat of arms of Queen Elizabeth II.

It is extremely doubtful whether Wytham Abbey ever was an abbey: there seems to have been a nunnery once, but as it was reputedly deserted during the 8th century during a war between Mercia and Wessex, there seems little justification in the title. The house was built in the sixteenth century by the Harcourts, and was remodelled by the same Earl of Abingdon who rebuilt the church, using this time the materials of a house at Rycote, in Oxfordshire. The Earls of Abingdon were members of the Bertie family, one of whom, Montague Bertie, had been a prominent supporter of Charles I and fought for him at Newbury, Cropredy, Lostwithiel and Naseby, where he was wounded, and died in 1666. The third Earl was he who resurrected the church brasses; the fourth, Willoughby Bertie, was a radical Whig who supported the rakish John Wilkes, the American colonists in their War of Independence, the Irish in their struggle against the British government, and the French revolutionaries, opposing Britain's war against them. The fifth Earl, another Montague, preferred playing with bricks and stones rather than with politics and fire: he was the church and house builder.

The last extremity of the Wytham peninsula is a flat stretch of farmland extending to the bend of the river, and presided over by the University Field Station. Down by the Seacourt Stream a short way from the Field Station is a farmstead and the fragmentary remains of Godstow Nunnery. It was a Benedictine nunnery, founded in the first year of King Stephen's reign, 1135 (its name means 'place dedicated to the service of God') and remarkable only for its connection with Henry II's almost legendary mistress, Rosamund Clifford. No contemporary writer mentions her by name in this connection, but Gerald of Wales, at the end of the century, says that Henry, after having imprisoned his wife Eleanor (for having encouraged his sons to rebel against him) began to live in open adultery with someone, and the nearest Gerald goes to giving her name is a pun on her name: '*. . . non mundi quidem rosa . . . sed in mundi verius rosa . . .*'. Subsequent writers speak of her having been hidden from the Queen's jealousy at the King's palace at Woodstock, in a secret chamber 'of Daedalian workmanship' and that she died soon after the King had openly acknowledged her and was buried in the chapter-house at Godstow. The burial was confirmed by later writers and the nunnery was endowed by Rosamund's father, Walter de Clifford, and by Henry, for the good of Rosamund's soul. Leland says that her tomb was broken up at the Reformation. The stories about the dagger and the poison cup are part of the legend, based on no known fact.

If it is hard to reach Wytham and Godstow from the direction of Cumnor, it is worse still to get back again by a different route. There is a footpath, which leaves the lane to the Field Station at right angles and thereafter sticks to the edge of the forest which covers Wytham Hill all the way round to its north-western side, but it is often obscure and usually hard going. Wytham Great Wood rears up over the hill with impenetrable density, a trackless wilderness; the path reaches the river, here called Isis, quite narrow and entirely rural, and struggles along its bank, still under the hanging vastness of the dim, mysterious woods. At last they curve away up the hill and the path follows the river to Swinford Lock, where there is a graceful stone bridge with a balustrade.

It is now necessary to take the long trail back to Cumnor and the North Berkshire Ridge for the completion of this stage of the tour. Not far from Swinford and still in sight of Wytham Hill there is a huge reservoir at Farmoor, on which work is still in progress although it was first filled in 1967; once on the Ridge there are very agreeable views to either side, to the Vale of White Horse on the left and to the Oxfordshire hills beyond the river on the right. Appleton, along the Ridge, is only half a mile from the church at Besselsleigh: it was from the Besils, by marriage, that its manor was first acquired by the Fettiplaces, and it was from Appleton that this family generated its complex web of connections all over the villages of North Berkshire.

The first known Fettiplace was Adam, who was Mayor of Oxford in 1240, and even by that time the manor-house at Appleton, parts still existing, had been built. Sir Nikolaus Pevsner calls it 'an amazing survival', because it is part of a manor-house built at the end of the twelfth century (when Gerald of Wales was writing his cryptic reference to Rosamund Clifford, and Richard Coeur de Lion was King of England). The sixteenth-century Fettiplaces remodelled it in the current fashion, and it is that combination of Tudor and late Norman which can be seen today, although it is difficult for the passing traveller to catch more than a passing glimpse from the churchyard. There is also an ancient barn, nearer the road, which is plain to see, and the church is basically of the same date as the old manor-house. There are no more Fettiplaces, however, in the house: the last one, George, died of apoplexy in the Bull Inn, Burford, on his way back from the races, in 1805.

Appleton, like all the Ridge villages, is built of stone: so is the hamlet Netherton and so, on the south-facing slope of the Ridge, is Fyfield.

The normal holding of a thegn (equivalent to the Norman lord of the manor) in Anglo-Saxon England was five hides, and this simple denomination of land is the origin of the name Fyfield. In 956 it was land *'aet fif hidum'*; in 968, *'aet Fifhidan'*, and in Domesday Book it had reached Fivehide. What, then, was a hide? 'However unwilling', says the great F. W. Maitland, 'we may be to face this dreary old question, we cannot escape it.' That it was a quantity of land is clear, but what quantity? 'Between the advocates of big hides of 120 acres or thereabouts and the advocates of little hides of 30 acres or thereabouts there should be no peace.' Like most other named areas of land, it had its origin in the need for an even assessment for purposes of taxation. 'Let it be granted that, long before the Norman conquest, the hide has become an unit in an unwieldy system of taxation . . . until the fiscal hide in a given case may widely diverge from its original or indeed from any fixed type. None the less, this system has for its base the theory that the typical man of Anglo-Saxon law, the typical householder or taxpayer, has a hide, has land enough for a team of oxen, has 120 arable acres.'

The manor-house of Fyfield is not as old either as the allotment of the five hides, nor even as old as its neighbour at Appleton, but it does date from the early fourteenth century, even if it does not look any more venerable than its Elizabethan front and grey-stone wing. It is a stone house of about 1320 complete with hall, porch and service wing, only the solar wing lacking. There is now in front of it a timber-framed gable, a great window, and the Tudor wing standing tall and grey behind it. It might have been occupied, but was certainly not built, by Sir John Golafre, lord of the manor, who died in 1442 and is buried in the church close by: his tomb, described by Pevsner as a 'terrifying representation', has an effigy of Sir John above and of his skeleton below. In his will Sir John left money for the foundation of a chantry house or hospital, to be occupied by a chantry priest (to say masses for Sir John's soul) and five almsmen. Sir John's executors duly built the house, a hundred yards south of the church, and there it still is, as the White Hart inn, its central room as open from floor to rafters (after restoration) as it was when the priest and five almsmen moved in.

The church at Fyfield was badly damaged by a fire in 1893, and the rebuilding left it with a rather lop-sided appearance and a little octagonal tower. The porch, with its two ear-like pinnacles, was an earlier Victorian addition of 1868. The building dates mainly from the late twelfth century. An unexpected memorial in it is Lady Katherine Gordon's: romantically dubbed the White Rose of Scotland, she was unromantically humiliated because, a cousin of

3 *above* Wayland's Smithy; 4 *below* The Ridgeway near Letcombe Bassett

King James IV of Scotland, she had been given in marriage to a good-looking young fellow who was currently (in the 1490's) posing as Richard IV of England, an episode which throws considerable doubt on the Tudor version of the 'Princes in the Tower' story, since this man - Perkin Warbeck - was pretending to be one of them. When Warbeck was imprisoned and finally executed, Lady Katherine resumed her maiden name, remained unmarried for some 11 years, and eventually received a grant of land in Berkshire, some of which was at Fyfield. She then married, successively, three gentlemen, all in the service of the King, and received from each more land and more wealth. She died in 1537 and was buried in Fyfield church, in preference to the fine tomb that her third husband, Sir Matthew Cradock, had prepared for both of them in Swansea.

5 *above* Bisham Abbey; 6 *below* Buscot Park

TWO

Isis

I have chosen the name of the Upper Thames for this chapter heading, because it forms the northern boundary of the chapter limits from Newbridge, where the A415 crosses it, to St John's Bridge, where the A417 goes off to Lechlade in Wiltshire. The southern boundary is the A420 road, which allows an extension to the western triangle bordered by the little River Cole, the boundary with Wiltshire. The name Isis has nothing to do with an Egyptian deity: it is probably yet another corruption of the Celtic word *uisge,* which simply means water: other examples are the rivers called Ouse, Esk, Usk, Axe and Exe, and the drink whisky, from *uisge beatha,* which means precisely the same as *aqua vitae.*

Geographically we are concerned here with the land that slopes gently southwards from the Isis, then rises suddenly to the Ridge, on which stand most of the villages of the region, and the quite high hills between Faringdon and the Cole.

Only a mile separates Fyfield, where the last chapter finished, and Kingston Bagpuize, on the A415 and A420 where they cross. As in the case of a great many villages with double names, the two elements are, respectively, Anglo-Saxon and Norman. Kingston means what it says, a tun or manor belonging to the King; Bagpuize (pronounced by twentieth-century villagers Bag-pews) is the name of a very early post-Conquest holder of the manor, whom Domesday Book calls Ralph de Bachepuz, who came from Bacquepuis in Normandy. By 1921 it had already been rendered Baggepus, so the modern version is an improvement on that. As a village it suffers somewhat from being crossed four ways by such eminent thoroughfares, and has plenty of new houses for people who do not mind incessant noise, but it does have a little green, a pleasing little classically-styled church of 1800, a great tall Georgian Kingston House, of 1720, with a central pedimented block of three bays and three storeys, and an excellent inn, the Hind's Head. Behind the grounds of the House, in a sports field, is a grassy declivity called Aelfrith's Ditch, which can be seen from the road to Abingdon. It is, as its name suggests, a Saxon earthwork, presumably constructed to defend the King's tun at some obscure time.

The first village on the Ridge, north-west from Kingston Bagpuize, is Longworth, which is famous for growing roses, although when I visited it, in the uncommonly dry summer of 1976, they were no more luxuriant than any other flower. It is quite a large village, with no shortage of very attractive stone cottages, with a tiny Primitive Methodist chapel of 1861 which is no longer used, and a bigger Congregational one of 1848, which is, and the church and manor-house group up a lane to the west, away from the main part. The Civil War of the seventeenth century plays an important part in Berkshire history, and Longworth contributed a prominent participant to both sides. In the village still is Marten's Hall Farm, principal seat of Sir Henry Marten, an eminent judge in the time of James I. His son Harry, who according to John Aubrey was 'a great lover of pretty girls, to whom he was so liberal that he spent the greatest part of his estate', was Member of Parliament for Berkshire in both the Short and Long Parliaments of 1640, and since King Charles I thought him 'an ugly rascal' and a 'whore-master' and had him turned out of Hyde Park, he became a keen, extreme and outspoken Parliamentarian. When the time came to put the captured King on trial, Marten sat regularly as one of the judges, and was a signatory of the death-warrant. Most of the surviving regicides, after the Restoration, were arrested, tried and executed, but Marten, who must have mellowed considerably in later years, had often intervened on behalf of persecuted Royalists during the interregnum years, and was spared execution: he spent the rest of his life (he died in 1680, at 78) in prison. Aubrey's verdict on him is charitable.

Longworth's contribution to the King's cause was Dr John Fell, son of Dr Samuel, Dean of Christ Church and Rector of Sunningwell. Born at Longworth, he was in 1643, at the age of 18, already a Master of Arts and in arms for the King, in the Oxford garrison. With his father, he was ejected from the University by the Parliamentary visitation of 1648, but joined the band of clergymen who, throughout the Commonwealth period, did their best to maintain Church of England services and standards in Oxford; this activity ensured rapid promotion for him at the Restoration, and Fell too became Dean of Christ Church, and in six years Vice-Chancellor of the University. He was one of those creatures who, impatient of intolerance in others, becomes equally intolerant in turn: he insisted on full conformity, in all students, with the Church of England, and returned the University to the conditions of Laud's days. He conducted examinations himself, attended all disputations for higher degrees, and was a stickler for discipline. Small wonder that Tom Brown, himself later on Dean of Christ Church, while an undergraduate in Fell's time as Dean, wrote this parody of Thomas Forde's translation of Martial's '*Non amo te, Sabidi . . .*':

I do not love thee, Doctor Fell,
The reason why I cannot tell;
But this I know, and know full well:
I do not love thee, Doctor Fell.

St Mary's Church, Longworth, bears evidence of construction in the thirteenth century, in some of its arches and windows, but was rebuilt in the fifteenth century in the prevalent Perpendicular style. There are two fifteenth-century brasses and one of 1566, and a modern one to its most celebrated rector (and certainly one of its longest-serving: 32 years) Dr John Richardson Illingworth. He was an intellectual, a writer on theology, and entertained for many years at Longworth a group of like-minded clergymen who became known as the *Lux Mundi* group, after a collection of essays with that title, published in 1889. They constituted one of the fresh breezes that the Church needs from time to time to blow away old misconceptions and attitudes by some serious and objective thinking. There are several features in the church at Longworth, such as the 'Arts and Crafts' east window, the pulpit, and the memorial brass, which are tributes to Dr Illingworth's life and work.

The manor-house, a tall and elegant stone house, stands in the accustomed position of manor-houses, next to the church; its name-plate, on the drive wall, looks remarkably like the name-plate of an old locomotive on the Great Western Railway. A footpath cuts across the fields a short half-mile to Hinton Waldrist, which stands on a 'height' of 290 feet, higher than most of the Ridge. This geographical fact is registered in the Anglo-Saxon element of its name, which means 'tun on high land'; the second element, as usual, is from one of its earlier lords of the manor. In 1192 it was held by Thomas de St Walerico, from St Val´ery in France. There is in the dense woods which surround the manor-house (an eighteenth-century building with some surviving details of the seventeenth century) an earthwork which is the motte of a twelfth-century motte-and-bailey castle. A moat still exists around the manor-house. There is an even earlier (by more than a thousand years) earthwork in an equally thick copse on nearby Windmill Hill, a rectangle with a single bank and ditch, possibly from the 1st century, A.D. The significant factor in the choice of this place for defensive works is the superior height overlooking both the Isis valley and the Vale of White Horse, one on either side. The church stands against a background of the high trees, which screen all these curiosities from the passer-by.

A good impression can be obtained of the commanding height on which these fortifications stand by taking the lane that leads northwards from the church down to the river plain where Duxford Farm sits in its windy isolation. From here a difficult, rather hypothetical footpath crosses a series of arable fields until it comes within sight of Buckland, back on the Ridge.

At first sight from the struggles across the cornfields to find the correct path, Buckland looks like one of Vauban's French fortresses, because of the barrack-like front of the stone range next to the battlemented church tower. It looks like the usual church-and-manor-house group and, in fact, was before Sir Robert Throckmorton in 1757 caused a greater mansion, more fitting to a gentleman of his social standing, to be built at a short distance away. The old manor-house, which was built about 1600, was abandoned and then turned into stables for the mansion, but had first to undergo a conversion, with pointed window-arches, into the currently fashionable Gothick style. It appears now to be a house again.

The church was repaired extensively in the seventeenth century, which explains the plainness of the tripartite windows, but there are still features of its early twelfth-century origin: the south doorway, and the high round-headed windows in the nave, for example. It has a crossing tower, with transepts: the north one remains fairly pure Early English (thirteenth-century), but the south transept is a splendid example of High Victorian, like the Albert Chapel in Windsor Castle, all colours of the rainbow. There is a little Jacobean wooden gallery on the nave side of the tower-crossing, some hatchments (coats of arms on diamond-shaped boards) on the ceiling, some big seventeenth-century monuments, one to Sir Edward Yate, who has in his arms some gates ('y' and 'g' are often exchangeable in old English script) and brasses to earlier Yates, who were lords of the manor.

Buckland village is compact and very pretty, all in stone like the other Ridge villages, and far enough from the A420 road to be peaceful. Buckland House can be seen from the lane going westward from the village, opposite the sports field. It is a magnificent square classical mansion, three storeys in stone, with just a hint of Palladio to denote the eighteenth-century gentleman's cultural taste. The two wings, octagonal rotunda-shaped, were added in 1910. The Throckmorton family, one of whom built the mansion, sprang from Sir George Throckmorton of Coughton in Warwickshire, who had eight sons (large families usually resulted in a far-flung network of connections). The house used to contain the celebrated Throckmorton Coat, but this is housed in Newbury Museum, so will be described in the appropriate section. It now bears the title University Hall.

A footpath from the end of the lane from Buckland leads to Carswell Manor, a big Victorian house in Tudor style, based on an early seventeenth-century wing, which can be detected by the windows. Very few manor-houses of any size are still private residences: this one is a school.

Littleworth, still going westwards, is a small village with many of its stone houses from the 1880-1890 period, and if a way is wanted of getting to Radcot Bridge without going into Faringdon and out on main roads, then there is a remarkably long and plumbline-straight lane from Littleworth down from the Ridge to the river plain. It does a violent L-turn after more than a mile of undeviating directness, by the farmstead of Thrupp, and meets the north-bound A4095 from Faringdon; a short length of this reaches the Isis, a little island in it where the stream divides, and Radcot Bridge. It is a good mediaeval bridge, with three ribbed arches, the first and third of which are pointed and had quite possibly been built when a short engagement took place in the water-meadows to its north-west, in 1387.

Richard II, son of the Black Prince, suffered from having come to the throne while still a boy: he was obliged to let his uncles and senior barons rule for him, and these dignitaries tended not to relinquish their government nor to acknowledge that, at 20, the King had grown up. The Lords and Commons in Parliament, with references to what had happened to the King's great-grandfather Edward II, demanded the removal of his friend and Chancellor Michael de la Pole, impeached him for corruption, and foisted on the King a guiding council of uncles, lords and bishops. Richard refused to submit to this indignity, and as soon as Parliament rose he reinstated Pole and set off to rally support in the Midlands. The royal judges in Nottingham declared that Parliamentary action without the King's approval was illegal and the authors of it therefore criminals. Richard felt reassured by this support of his authority, and collected an army in Cheshire. His uncle the Duke of Gloucester and other leading earls also raised an army in London for defence; they met the King in Westminster Hall and once again asserted their overbearing personalities over the uncertain young King. He was obliged to agree again to the impeachment of his favourites, de la Pole and Robert de Vere, Earl of Oxford, and to call a Parliament for February 1388. In the meantime de Vere raised another army in Cheshire (a royal earldom) and marched towards London, meaning to cross the Thames at Radcot Bridge. But the Duke of Gloucester, joined by Henry Bolingbroke, Earl of Derby, the King's cousin, surprised de Vere (who had recently been created Duke of Ireland by the King) by crossing the river and meeting him on the northern bank. According to Jean Froissart, the chronicler, de Vere and de la Pole who was with him, being frightened of the consequences of being captured by the opposition, planned to bolt. 'We had better place ourselves on one of the wings . . . and so we shall have two strings to our bow. We shall be able to see how our men are doing. If they are fighting well we will stay, for the honour of the King who sent us here. If they are defeated, we will get away across country and have the advantage of being free to ride in whichever direction we choose.'

The Duke of Gloucester's party 'came in warlike order with their banners unfurled, amid a great sounding of trumpets. When the King's men saw them, their courage forsook them. They broke formation and began to disperse and take to their heels. Word had gone round that their commander, the Duke of Ireland, was running away with his lieutenants. So they fled in all directions, without attempting to resist.' That was the end of the Battle of Radcot Bridge: the Duke of Gloucester gave orders that no-one should be killed except in self-defence, and few were, except some trampled in the crush. It wrecked the King's position: the 'Merciless' Parliament of 1388 exiled or executed all the King's friends. The King began a long period of learning how to live with his enemies, biding his time, until in 1397, ten years after Radcot Bridge, he turned on them.

It is always difficult to assess, in the Middle Ages, the affections of the populace on any matter, because they were never consulted and had no means of registering an opinion. It is, however, a fact, and may not be entirely a coincidence, that in this region of North Berkshire there is a disproportionate number of inns bearing the sign of the White Hart: and the White Hart was the personal badge of King Richard II.

The fields where the so-called battle was enacted are still quite uncluttered with building, as are the meadows on the near side. The Isis here is quite narrow but still used by holiday motor-cruisers, and very inviting with willows lining the banks. A tenuous and uncertain footpath is alleged to take one across the fields to Camden Farm and then on to Eaton Hastings, but judging by the fact that it does not appear to exist at all except in a series of vaguely connected stiles and gates, no-one has used it for a long time.

Eaton Hastings is a tiny, lonely hamlet, close by the river. Its name means 'tun on a river', and it was held by Ralph de Hastinges in 1161, and its parish area is actually quite extensive, so here we have a mediaeval shrunken village. The church, Norman and thirteenth-century in origin, is small, so possibly there never were very many inhabitants. There is a field south of the church which has a curiously irregular surface: under it might possibly lie the foundations or remains of some earlier cottages. There is no manor-house. There are several reasons for the diminution or removal of a village, and the one that comes to mind in this case is the Plague: not necessarily the Black Death, although that was the most destructive, but any outbreak of pestilence could have the effect of wiping out a small community, and return to an infected area would naturally be reluctant.

Buscot, the next parish to Eaton Hastings, has the distinction of being the last in this north-western corner of old Berkshire: in fact the other side of the Isis here belongs to Wiltshire, so even as modern Oxfordshire it is an extremity. In Domesday Book it appears as *Boroardescote,* and in a cartulary of 1130 as *Burwardescota*: it represents a man's name, Burgweard's cot. It too has moved away from its church, which is on the banks of the Isis: early riverside settlements were often abandoned when roads began to grow in importance with more traffic on them, especially when they were turnpiked during the course of the eighteenth century. Buscot village today clusters around a street off the A417 road from Faringdon to Lechlade; it has a little village hall by the main road, with a clock tower and a written commemoration of Queen Victoria's Golden Jubilee, a covered well, which still has a standpipe and tap which functions, and several cottages of the 1890s, all built for Sir Alexander Henderson, later Lord Faringdon, of Buscot House.

James Dugdale, who published Volume I of his *New British Traveller* in 1819, says that Buscot House 'forms a conspicuous object from the Faringdon road', and that the Park, of about 150 acres, was a farm which had been bought back by a Mr Edward Lovedon after having been out of his family for 150 years. The house was built in the 1770s, and is neither conspicuous nor even visible from the Faringdon road nowadays, because of all the trees, which were no doubt planted by the aforesaid Mr Lovedon. Lord Faringdon held socialist views, while behaving with the charitable benevolence of any good estate-owner, and seems to have been in touch with Morris and the 'Arts and Crafts' movement, since the house contains Burne-Jones's 'Sleeping Beauty' series, and the church has windows by him. He also bred Shire horses, one of which, Buscot Harold, was champion three years running, at the turn of the century, at the London Shire Horse Show.

Lord Faringdon took his title from the little town which stands at the junction of five important highways, the roads (clockwise) to Witney, to Oxford, to Wantage, to Swindon, and to Cirencester. In these days of motorways and airports, such a position does not necessitate vital importance (only traffic-jams) but before the advent of such modern delights of transport, in other words throughout 99.9% of the town's history, it certainly did. Enough importance, at any rate, for the Parliamentary troops in the Civil War to besiege it for four years, hoping to gain control of the junction, and for the Royalists to hang on to it like grim death.

To begin with, the kings of Wessex are reputed to have had a palace there. This has been said of a number of west-country towns, and is difficult to establish because Anglo-Saxon palaces were built of wood and traces of them turn up only infrequently and often by accident. King Edward the Elder, the great Alfred's son, is said to have died in this one: perhaps he did, but the Anglo-Saxon Chronicle states quite explicitly that he died in Farndon-on-Dee in Mercia, and his son Aelfweard 16 days later at Oxford, and that they were both buried at Winchester. Farndon and Faringdon are both derived from *Fearndun,* a fern-clad hill, so the confusion is no doubt understandable.

What is indisputable is that there was a castle mound erected nearby in the twelfth century, on the hill called Folly Hill, and that one may safely assume that it was the one that Robert, Earl of Gloucester, defended against King Stephen. Robert was one of Henry I's numerous bastards: like Charles II he was rather better at begetting children out of holy wedlock than in it. Robert took the part of his half-sister Maud against her cousin Stephen, during the unfortunate period known as the Anarchy. It was really another civil war, rather than anarchy, despite what the Anglo-Saxon Chronicle says, because the situation came about through a disputed claim to the throne: Maud was certainly Henry I's daughter, but the idea of a woman ruler was not universally popular (among the landowners: no-one bothered what anyone else thought) and furthermore she had married the Count of Anjou, the traditional enemy of Normandy. If the resulting chaos was anarchy, then so was the York-and-Lancaster struggle and so was the attempt by Charles I to assert his authority against a rebellious parliament. Stephen's siege of Robert's castle at Faringdon in 1145, achieved in four days (Robert may not have been there), was one of his greatest successes because it isolated his opponents' stronghold at Wallingford and kept them in check in the west country.

The hill on which the castle mound was thrown up is crowned by a copse of pine trees, called the Folly, planted by one Henry Pye, Poet Laureate, of whom more later. Above the trees there peep the top-most crenellations of a tower, another folly to add to Pye's, which Lord Berners had erected in 1935. It must be one of the last of the architectural follies.

All Saints Church, Faringdon, is exceptionally fine. It stands at the top of a little rise from the Market Place, above a sloping churchyard bank, and has an almost entirely Norman nave, with characteristic little round-headed clerestory windows. The chancel, nearly as long as the nave, is Early English, with equally characteristic slender lancet windows. The tower, low and flat, is between the two sections, and is reduced in size (it once had a spire) because it was damaged during the siege by Parliamentary troops. One of the monuments in the church is to a typically Elizabethan soldier-diplomatist-scholar, Sir Henry Unton, a contemporary and friend of Sir Philip Sidney, and cast in the same mould.

Unton was born at Wadley House, a little further to the east from Folly Hill, second son of Sir Edward Unton, of an old Berkshire family. His mother, Anne, had a startlingly lurid background, not through her own fault: her father, Edward Seymour, Duke of Somerset, her husband, John Dudley, Earl of Warwick, and her father-in-law, John Dudley, Duke of Northumberland, had all come to a sudden end on the block, all within 18 months of one another. Her second marriage must have seemed like a safe harbour after a tempest at sea.

Henry graduated from Oxford in his teens, studied law at Middle

Temple, and in his mid-20s was elected Member of Parliament for New Woodstock. The next year, 1585, having found favour with the Lord Chancellor, Sir Christopher Hatton, who commended him to the Queen, he went with the Earl of Leicester's army to the Netherlands to help the Protestant Dutch in their struggle against their Spanish overlords. At Zutphen, where his friend Sir Philip Sidney behaved with such splendid chivalry, he too distinguished himself but survived, and was knighted by Leicester. In 1591 Unton was appointed ambassador to King Henry IV of France, and seems to have discharged his office rather more enthusiastically than many ambassadors, since he troubled to attend the King when he was in action with his armies, at Rouen in 1591 and at Aumale, where the King was wounded, the next year. In the spring of that year he heard that the young Duke of Guise had spoken 'impudently, lightly and overboldly' of Queen Elizabeth, and in the best traditions of chivalry he issued a challenge to the Duke to meet him with whatever arms he chose, on horse or on foot. The 'bold' Duke declined, even though Unton re-issued the challenge three times.

Unton had to return home, ill, in 1593, but was sent to France again to the much-admired Henry, who was still engaged in struggles against Spain. While Unton was with him at the siege of La Fère on the upper Oise he caught 'a purple fever' and died, in 1596. He was buried in Faringdon church.

Close to the churchyard gate there is a pair of fine gate-piers, standing at the entrance to the drive of Faringdon House. They are survivors of the rebuilding of the house after the Civil War, when it was the centre of a stout Royalist resistance. One odd circumstance came when it was besieged by its owner.

Robert Pye was knighted by James I in 1621 and bought the manor of Faringdon from the Untons; he represented Woodstock in the Long Parliament and stayed in it all through the war. His son, another Robert, married John Hampden's daughter and in 1642 raised a troop of horse for Parliament. He fought with distinction all the way through the conflict with the King, and in May 1646 was detached by Fairfax from the siege of Bristol to command the besieging forces at Faringdon, which had been defended by Sir Marmaduke Rawdon for the King with such obstinacy. When

Oxford surrendered, on 24 June 1646, so did Faringdon.

The house was rebuilt after the war, but when a descendant of Sir Robert called Henry James Pye succeeded to the estate, the house, and debts of £50,000, he was further burdened when the house burned down. The present Faringdon House had to wait 14 years before the unfortunate Pye could begin it, and it was still not finished five years later, in 1785.

This Henry Pye played his part as a Member of Parliament (for Berkshire), but his real aim in life was to gain recognition as a poet. This was distinctly unfortunate, because although he was a scholar and could write English verse, no-one, on reading it, could with justification call it poetry. Certainly none of his comtemporaries did, and when William Pitt, either from sardonic humour or because he cared nothing for poetry, as a reward to Pye for parliamentary support created him Poet Laureate, he could hardly have debased the post more if he had given it to his horse. He held it for 23 years until he died in 1813, and never produced anything more exciting than 'Faringdon Hill', a stanza from which follows:

'Here lofty mountains lift their azure heads,
There its green lap the grassy meadow spreads:
Enclosures here the sylvan scene divide,
There plains extended spread their harvest wide.
Here oaks their massy limbs wide stretching meet,
And form impervious thickets at our feet.
Through aromatic heaps of rip'ning hay,
There silver Isis wins her winding way;
And many a bower, and many a spire between,
Shoots from the groves and cheers the rural scene.'

As Dugdale tactfully puts it, the lines give 'an interesting and correct picture of this beautiful scene' if they give nothing much else.

The Market Place in Faringdon is at the meeting of the highways; the Bell and the Crown face each other across it with Georgian frontages, although the Crown reputedly has some fourteenth-century remnants behind that façade, and in between them is the little Town Hall, all on columns, built in the late seventeenth century like the one at Abingdon, but unlike it in every other respect: this is a much homelier hall. Next to the Crown is a lopsided building, also of the seventeenth century, and the town is full of good Georgian houses.

Little Coxwell, a mile or so south of Faringdon, is really the wrong side of the A420 properly to qualify for this chapter, but in all other respects it belongs to it, so it may be included. A shady lane slips away from the busy Swindon road and, as so often in this country, is almost traffic-less. Little Coxwell lies between it and the main road and the first building to be seen is a graceful early Georgian house of about 1720, in brick, with three elliptical windows over the porch and two wings: this is Church House, and behind it among the trees is the simple little stone church, St Mary's, which consists of a Norman nave and chancel and a good late thirteenth-century bellcote between the two. Most of the windows are Perpendicular, there are porches on both sides, and hanging between them inside is a huge brass chandelier of 1729. At the west end there is a gallery with the remains of the old rood screen. The village is small and compact, all in stone and as pretty as those on the Ridge. On a nearby hill where Ringdale Manor stands there is a small Iron Age hill-fort, one of several on the southward slopes of this region, facing the Downs: more will be said about them later.

To go through Little Coxwell back to the main road, cross it and take a footpath across a field, is a quick way to its neighbouring twin, Great Coxwell, which is somewhat larger and of a slightly different character. The footpath slips between two of the stone cottages and joins the street, and from the churchyard a little way along to the left it can be seen that the village, still in stone, is on several levels on a hillside and has something of the look of one of those wonderful Provençal villages, except that it is considerably less dilapidated. The church is larger than Little Coxwell's, aptly enough, but basically of the same late Norman date. It has an early thirteenth-century chancel and a Perpendicular tower.

At the end of the village, going north away from the church, there is a farm with a delightful and graceful late seventeenth-century stone farmhouse. In front of it there is a duckpond, and beyond that there is one of the most remarkable and fascinating buildings in all Berkshire. It is a huge barn, and it was built by the Cistercian monks of Beaulieu Abbey, in Hampshire, in the early thirteenth century.

King John has generally had, as the saying goes, a bad press. He was not the most amiable of characters, but he was only trying to rule as his brother and father had done, in increasingly difficult circumstances, some of which tended to bring out the worst in him. He was keenly interested in law and the meting out of justice to his subjects, and he was not at all irreligious, as he is often accused of being. When, therefore, in 1200, he heard the complaints of twelve Cistercian abbots against his own forest officials (who were apt to be extremely overbearing) he offered not only to redress their grievances, but to build them a new abbey too. He gave them land and the means for building, and endowed the new Beaulieu Abbey with many manors for the monks' upkeep. One of the manors was at Great Coxwell, and the monks built there a barn in which to store all the produce that was brought to them as tithes, or rent.

The barn, like most other buildings of this region, is of stone, and stone-slated, is 152½ feet long and 51 feet high, with air-vents at regular intervals in its walls; its roof timbers are supported by two rows of mighty upright timber columns and these rest on solid stone piers. The timbers have been repaired and strengthened, but from its beaten earth floor to its lofty dim roof the barn gives an extraordinary impression of what any mediaeval building, church or hall, monastic or utilitarian, actually looked like at the time. It would be dark, there would be draughts everywhere, and in winter it would be very, very cold.

The National Trust cares for the great barn, contributions are welcome, pictures and literature are available, but it still functions as a store for goods used or produced by the farm.

A stiff climb from the barn to a height of about 500 feet half a mile further on arrives at Badbury Clumps. It is the highest hill for many a mile around, and it is no surprise to find that among the trees there are the ditches and ramparts of a contour hill-fort of the Iron Age. The view is panoramic, of the Downs to the south, Salisbury Plain to the south-west and the Cotswolds to the north-west. The men who made the fort chose the strongest position in the area; across the Vale of White Horse it faces another commanding height topped by an equally dominant fort, and in the next chapter when I come to discuss Uffington Castle and the White Horse itself, I intend also to return to the mysteries and possibilities of the other hill-forts, like Badbury.

On the next, lower hill, westwards, there is a crescent-shaped plantation of beeches called Cuckoo Pen, opposite the walls of Coleshill Park. Nearby are the seventeenth-century gate-piers guarding an entrance drive to the Park, but the big house itself is not there. It is a pity that it is not there, because by repute it was the best example in England of a mid-seventeenth-century house in the style of Inigo Jones. It was built between 1650 and 1662 for Sir George Pratt by his cousin Roger Pratt, in consultation with Jones. One of its features was a most beautiful staircase. Unfortunately in 1952 it was gutted by fire, and the ruins were demolished: only the gate-piers and a dovecot remain. It was for a while the seat of the Bouverie family, Earls of Radnor, a fact which is commemorated by the inn, the Radnor Arms, in the village.

Coleshill lies upon a steep descent to the River Cole; its church is about halfway down, and it looks rather odd, all tower and porch, because it was badly restored and has a very low nave roof, as if it were temporarily repaired after fire-damage. The Cole, the county boundary with Wiltshire, is a narrow, shallow stream, bridged in one arch.

There is a footpath through Coleshill Park which purports on the map to lead to Strattenborough Castle Farm, but it is guarded by an implacable gremlin which, unless knowledgeably propitiated by suitable sacrifices and libations, will either alter or totally obliterate the course of the path, so that the pilgrim is thrown wildly out of his way and must needs, licking his wounds, abandon the quest. If the right sop can be found to throw to this Cerberus, then Strattenborough Castle Farm is apparently worth seeing, not so much for the farmhouse itself, which is a late eighteenth-century mock-Gothick affair, but for one of its barns which has a genuine eleventh-century tympanum in a Danish Viking style. How it got there is by no means clear.

The sight from a vantage point on the A420 of the approaches to Watchfield and Shrivenham is not encouraging, because there is a mass of modern building and the Royal Military College of Science and little else to compensate for it, but Shrivenham has a church

7 *above* The Cistercian barn, Great Coxwell; 8 *below* The Abbey Guest House, Abingdon

entirely rebuilt in 1638 by Lord Craven, at a time when very few were built. In it are monuments to the Barrington family, one of whom was an admiral who distinguished himself in the numerous naval actions of the mid-eighteenth century, and the sole surviving relic of the earlier church, its late Norman font, in Purbeck marble.

From the same vantage point, in the vicinity of the lane that leads down to Longcot, there is a clear view of the queer-looking animal whose rangy, surrealistic lines are blazoned across one of the highest hills of the Downs. He looks like a war-banner, and that may be a clue to his purpose.

9 & 10 Sutton Courtenay: *above* The twelfth-century Hall; *below* All Saints' Church

THREE

The Vale Of White Horse

The lane from Longcot to the Downs passes by two examples of nineteenth-century enterprise, one which succeeded and is still functioning, and the other which was killed by the first. Between 1800 and 1830, following the commerical success of the great industrial canals of the north, canal companies were floated and began digging in all unlikely parts of the country. The Kennet and Avon Canal, engineered by John Rennie, connected with the already existing Newbury to Reading canal, was opened in 1810 and guaranteed instant profitability because of the bulk goods which could now be carried from London to Bristol. But the Berkshire and Wiltshire Canal, from Cirencester through the Vale of White Horse to the Thames at Abingdon was a different matter: it had to wriggle about like a demented snake and, when all was said and done, what vital industry with endless loads of bulk products or raw materials was going to use it? Agriculture, obviously, and as long as the canal was the only competitor in the field for its products, then its use was assured; so it was dug, and wound its tortuous course across the countryside, and throughout the Vale, from Shrivenham to Abingdon, it can be traced, a tree-lined ditch in the fields. But Brunel's Great Western Railway line opened, running trains along the same route with twenty times the rapidity of delivery. Bigger canals, if they were wide and deep enough and easy to navigate, could compete; the smaller ones collapsed, as the railways took over, because there was no commerical incentive to use them. By 1906 it was 'a waterless ditch, of some three years' standing as such'.

The lane from Longcot crosses the dead canal, then goes under a new bridge for the railway, and fast inter-city trains thunder overhead.

At Compton Beauchamp there are some strange old things. From the road up the hillside to it a lane leads to Hardwell Farm, which has a moat and was the site of some mediaeval dwelling: its name means 'hoard-spring', and not far away is the site of a villa from the Roman occupation. Was there, perhaps, a hoard of treasure hidden by the villa's occupants down the well? Some of the fields just north of Compton Beauchamp, by the roadside, bear the faint traces of the old strip-system: these are much more marked in fields by Denchworth and Charney Bassett so I will discuss them later in the chapter. Near the little church is its manor-house, Compton House, which is also moated: the house itself is part sixteenth-century but has an early eighteenth-century front. The house, the church, and many of the village cottages are built of chalk blocks. Chalk is a most unlikely building material, because it is soft and erosive, but these few villages north of the Downs used it, even for their churches, and they are still there. Part of the church dates from the early thirteenth century, when the village name was written 'Cumton Beucamp' and the manor was held by Walter de Bello Campo (Latin version of Beauchamp). Later, in 1273, the place is referred to as 'Cumpton near le Whitehors'.

The road from Compton Beauchamp along the lower slopes of the Downs to Ashbury is a section of one of two ancient trackways which run more or less parallel with one another, one on the crest of the hills, the other on the northern scarp-slope, all the way to the Thames. The lower is variously called the Icknield Way, and Ickleton Street, names which might appear to have a bearing on the Celtic tribe which occupied East Anglia in Roman times, the Iceni. It is found in 903 spelt *Iccenhilde weg,* and in 1185 *Ikenildestreta,* but Professor Ekwall, the compiler of the *Dictionary of English Place-names,* says that 'the etymology of the name has not been found'. He is not, very properly, given to guess-work.

Ashbury is in the same kind of geographical position as Compton Beauchamp, and the Icknield Way passes through it. The older cottages, mainly thatched, are of chalk, some with the chalk blocks mixed with sandstone. The newer houses are usually brick. The church is also built of chalk and parts of it certainly existed in the twelfth century because the south doorway is round-headed and has the characteristic dog-tooth moulding on the outside. A tablet in the chancel proclaims that here, in 1777, the Rev. Thomas Stock began a Sunday School, and that this was later the first to be housed in its own building outside. The manor-house, in chalk and stone like the church, is a rare survival from the fifteenth century: chalk, against all probabilities, appears to have lasted extremely well.

One of the shortest and least burdensome routes up to the top of the Downs is the lane from Ashbury, and within a mile, just over the crest, the second of the two ancient trackways, the Ridgeway, comes swooping down from the distant Wiltshire hills to cut across it at right angles. Here it is a pleasant wide green way, and walking along it, far more than walking along the lower track which is metalled as a modern road, gives a feeling of intense affinity with all the many people throughout all the centuries who have used it before.

Some of those who used the Ridgeway around 4000 years ago were the people of the New Stone Age who constructed the megalithic chambered long barrow known as Wayland's Smithy which lies just off it in this section. It stands on a high point of the Downs crest and so could have been seen from a great distance: it is now surrounded with a ring of beeches. Thirteen skeletons were discovered in this tomb, in a ridge-roofed enclosure of wood and stone, a barrow raised over it, and later the mound was enlarged by the digging of two flanking ditches and the construction of the chamber, from great sarsen stones, at its south end. More sarsens were used to shore up the sides of the barrow. It seems to be akin to a group of similar tombs of the Cotswold region, around the Severn estuary, and their builders are therefore known as people of the Severn culture, living around 2000 B.C.

The tomb has been known as Wayland's Smithy since at least 955 A.D. Wayland, in Scandinavian and Germanic mythology, was the equivalent of Hephaestus or Vulcan, the smith of the gods, and by tradition the owner of a white horse. It was therefore not surprising, that the West Saxons who settled hereabouts should connect the great stones of the chambered tomb with the white horse cut in the hillside, and conclude that the horse was Wayland Smith's and the tomb was his smithy. The story went around that a traveller whose horse cast a shoe only had to leave a coin on the capstone of the smithy to have his horse shod for him, since Wayland obviously made shoes for his own horse there.

A short way further along the Ridgeway approaches the twin phenomena of the great hill-fort, carved out of the highest point of the Downs, and the strange creature sprawled out in white chalk on the green north-facing slope, on the eastern shoulder of the hill. A great deal has been written about the horse to explain it, but since there is so little that can constitute empirical proof, most of it must necessarily be hypothesis.

What is known without dispute is what can be seen: that the figure is cut from the turf to expose the chalk, which shows in white contrast and can be seen from afar; that in its greatest length it measures 365 feet, it faces to the right, it has two legs connected with the body and two detached, and look as if they always have been, that it does not even look much like a horse; it is, as before suggested, a surrealistic impression of a horse, a work of art, which places it apart from any of the other chalk horses. It is something like the Celtic stylised animal-forms current in the 1st century B.C., which the Atrebates, who were a Belgic tribe invading and occupying the country south of the Thames from Berkshire to Hampshire, used on their coins. But the Atrebatic horses usually, for some reason, had three tails, and the White Horse has clean, sweeping lines of great simplicity, more akin to the art-forms of the late Bronze Age predecessors of the Belgae in its economy of lines. Also the fort on the hill above it is an early Iron Age fort and could possibly be contemporary with the horse (since the early Iron Age and the late Bronze Age overlapped: people of both cultures lived at the same time) and if that is the case they both preceded the Atrebates. That may be so, but the known facts are now giving way to cautious hypotheses, and a wider network of evidence may be brought in to support them.

There is a surprising number of Iron Age forts on the Downs and on both sides of them. There is no clear pattern, and Professor Frere, in *Britannia,* suggests that their proliferation indicates a period of lawlessness or anarchy, when each chieftain with his tribe and followers fortified his own most easily defensible hill-top because of aggressive marauders from other tribes. This seems the most likely explanation of the number in Berkshire and the Vale, although it is tempting to work on a theory that the Belgic Atrebates, who were certainly aggressive and arrived as a kind of warrior aristocracy as a result of the military activities of Caesar in Gaul, treated the Downs as their frontier to the north and from it breathed defiance. They lined the Downs with forts, periodically raided the settlements in the Vale, and carved their tribal symbol, the horse (which certainly appears on their coins), on the hillside below the strongest of their forts as an arrogant advertisement of their prowess. The forts on the northern side of the Downs would be constructed by the people, the Dobunni, whose territory extended to the Vale, which would account for the fact that one of them, Blewburton, is only fortified on the side that faces the Downs. Badbury would be the principal stronghold of the Dobunni in this region, intended to keep an eye on the Atrebates, and Sinodun, on the bend of the Thames by Little Wittenham, would watch any movements up the river from the gap in the hills.

It is a neat theory, but since neatness is not a characteristic attribute of history and confusion is, there is no sound reason for doubting Professor Frere's conclusion, that there were so many forts because there were so many hostile intruders and it was every man for himself and his family. And if the horse was carved by people before the Belgic invasions, it could not have been put there by the Atrebates, tribal symbol or not. But if it was not a nationalistic war-banner, what was it?

There is always the possibility of a religious significance: Celts, on the whole, however, seem to have worshipped spirits represented by sun, moon and stars, trees and rivers, rather than by animals or animal shapes. The Saxons evidently believed that it belonged to Wayland, and took great care to keep the outline clean: a scouring ceremony was held every seven years, the responsibility transferred in feudal times to the lord of the manor. Thomas Hughes described the last ceremony, in 1857, when everyone went up to the hill-fort, called Uffington Castle, and the lord of the manor had to entertain them and feed them for two days while the work of scouring the horse was carried out. There were booths, tents, side-shows, and all the fun of the fair. The Ancient Monuments Act relieved the lords of the manor (the Craven family) of the responsibility, and at once the seven-yearly scouring ceremony stopped. It must have looked and sounded much as it does on a hot afternoon in mid-summer nowadays, with cars parked a short distance away, people wandering all over the hillside, children running about screaming, and the kind of people who invariably fly kites on ancient monuments doing so from the heights of the hill-fort. Whether or not the White Horse pre-dates the Atrebates, I still feel that its connection with the fort is clear, and that it is a distinctive and defiant tribal symbol, like the eagle standards of the Roman army, or the insignia on a modern fighter aircraft.

Like any high place, it is easier to get down from the White Horse than it is to get up to it: a lane runs steeply down to the Icknield Way and from it can be seen not only the horse (although from close at hand its head is invisible) but the deep chasm before it, called the Manger, and the little conical hill slightly to its east called Dragon Hill. The legend of St George and the Dragon got mixed up with the horse at some point, to add to the confusion: it was sometimes held to be St George's horse, sometimes the Dragon. Like the holly, ivy and mistletoe and the Easter egg, pagan rites often got mixed up with Christian practices, and St George seems to have been identified with an earlier pagan horse-god, like the Wayland of the Saxons. Near Abergele in North Wales there is a well of Llan San Sior where until fairly recently horses were sacrificed to San Sior (St George). There is also the garbled folk-legend of the mummers' plays, with St George and the hobby-horse usually in prominent parts.

Another steep hill from the Icknield Way slides down into the delightful village of Woolstone, built mainly of chalk, with a little chalk church of Norman origin but later rebuilding, an array of chalk, thatched cottages, a fine timber-framed, brick-filled and tiled inn called (what else?) the White Horse, another good timber-framed cottage which could be quite early, close to a lovely gushing stream that comes from the Manger, and best of all a surprise piece: a three-storey pile of Victorian Byzantine extravagance in multi-coloured brick and chalk, marked clearly on the side 'A.N. 1877'.

Uffington is only a mile from Woolstone, but down on the flats of the Vale. There are some chalk cottages here as well, often bound with brick or stone or both. Where the road from Woolstone comes in, on a bank by the churchyard is a little square chalk building with mullioned, latticed windows, and the date 1617 over its door. This was the school; the new school, just round the corner, also next to the churchyard, has a new wing built of chalk blocks and roofed with stone slates, for which full marks should be given to the authority responsible. The church is mainly of the thirteenth century, but its crossing tower has an octagonal top storey added some time after 1740, and sundry other marks of restoration.

On the way to Kingston Lisle there is an otherwise unremarkable group of buildings called Fawler, a name which suggests that there might have been on the site a Roman house with a pavement, because Fawler is an old English word meaning floor, usually a threshing-floor, and used as a place-name may indicate some special kind of floor that existed when the first settlers arrived.

The Close Rolls of 1368-1369 record that *'Gerard de l'Isle tient en la Vale de White Horse 1 fee'*, a typically legal mixture of Norman-French and English which indicates that Gerard was possibly the first to add his name to that of the village, since in 1220 it is written simply as Kingston: another manor belonging to an early king. The village shelters under the lee of the Downs, since the road from Woolstone curves down to Uffington on the plain and then back again to the hills, and under the lee also of the high trees of Kingston Lisle House, an eighteenth-century gentleman's house with park and grounds and beautiful avenue of beeches, either side of the Icknield Way as it goes eastward from it. The little church of St John Baptist is of the late twelfth century, but has wall-paintings of the fourteenth and a good deal of dark woodwork, including the pulpit, of the seventeenth, all of which may be difficult to see because, when not in use, the church is kept locked.

These periods of church-building, such as the late twelfth century, the thirteenth, fifteenth, and all the restoration work and rebuilding of the nineteenth, occur at times of general national prosperity: under the firm government of Henry II and his circuit judges, under Henry III despite the complaints about his personal extravagance, even during the politically chaotic days of Henry VI when England's staple, the wool-trade, was reaching its heady heights of profitability, and certainly during the Victorians' 'Golden Age' when everything seemed to be going right. These were all times when the population was expanding, commerce was growing, energy and activity were encouraged, and wealthy folk, wishing partly to give as a Christian should and partly to show that they were wealthy, contributed funds towards rebuilding the local church. I do not hold with the cynical 'conspicuous consumption' theory to account for mediaeval church-building, but it has a partial basis in truth. At all events, the present wealth of mediaeval architecture we possess is certainly due to the commercial enterprise of our mediaeval ancestors. When they enjoyed a surplus, they gave it to the church.

A steep lane leads up to the Downs from Kingston Lisle, and on the left of it at the bottom there is a cottage, in the front garden of which there is, under a hollow old elm tree, an erect sarsen with holes in it. Some amiable Anglo-Saxon idiot in unrecorded times discovered that if he blew into the holes, it made a noise, since when the stone has been celebrated as the Blowing-Stone. The Downs, with the Ridgeway running along them, rear up behind the village, and there is another fort on the highest hill, called Ramsbury; it has been so ploughed out that it is unrecognisable as a fort, but after its original use by Iron Age Celts it seems to have been adapted in late Roman times. During the 4th century when the province was overrun by Picts and Scots in what seemed to be collusion (in 367) nothing was safe; many houses were burnt and it was quite possibly then that the hoard of silver coins was buried up there on the old fort, a refuge, perhaps, from the marauders.

Sparsholt is the adjoining parish eastwards from Kingston Lisle, on the slopes downhill from the old way: a cluster of cottages among the trees, an early Georgian (1722) manor-house and a small church with a shingled spire. It has a late Norman north doorway, with animal heads, and inside there are some fourteenth-century tombs with effigies of knights: the predominant architectural style is the Decorated one of the fourteenth century. There is a war memorial in the churchyard with a base of what looks like the stump of an old market cross.

The seventh, from west to east, of these Downland villages, is

Childrey: the reason for such a proliferation of settlements in this stretch of hilly country is a simple one, water. As a glance at the map will show, they are all situated where springs of water issue from the hillside. For most of them, parish boundaries extend northward to the arable plains of the Vale, and southward to the grazing land (nowadays also mostly arable) of the Downs. All the means of sustaining life were present.

Childrey is larger than most, strung out on the slope with the church at the bottom. It has a mixture of types of cottage, some stone, some brick, and some timber-framed with a mixture of the others, many thatched; there is a duckpond, a green with a war memorial, and a school originally founded by a Fettiplace, a branch of which family held the manor. The church is at the end of a lane at the end of the village, looking out over the Vale. The rectory is a big one with a huge garden (the rector used to be the largest landowner because over the years he acquired land from others in lieu of tithes) and there are in the garden some cedar trees which could well be the descendants of the one brought from Lebanon and planted on the lawn by Dr Pocock, who was rector in 1642. Alongside the church is a collection of stone farm buildings including a little round tower with a conical roof. The church itself is quite big, with chancel higher than nave, which is mainly thirteenth-century, as one may see from the arches. There is no chancel arch, but instead a wooden screen. On the left of the sanctuary there is a tomb with a stone canopy, of the late fourteenth century, called the Easter Sepulchre: the arch is ogee, which puts it into the early Perpendicular category. There is another, similar sepulchre in the north transept, with the effigy of a knight, in stone, and there are several brasses, one to an early sixteenth-century Fettiplace.

There is a lane opposite the turning to Childrey which starts off up the Downs scarp and forks, to Lambourn one way and to Letcombe Bassett the other. Lambourn belongs in another chapter. Letcombe Bassett shelters in a thickly wooded trough beneath the looming Downs and another hill-fort, Segsbury, also heavily disguised by foliage. This is a very small community, with an originally Norman, but largely restored (in 1861 by the famous Butterfield) church. Its name appears in 1212 as *Hledecumba,* from *hleda,* ledge, and *cumb,* a narrow valley; the manor was held by Richard Bassett in the mid-twelfth century. The spring which gave the settlement its incentive flows as the Letcombe Brook along the bottom of a deep defile, with many ponds, and followed by the road, to Letcombe Regis (a manor of the king). This is a much bigger village, depending on the Letcombe Brook and a tributary stream, with several good timber-framed cottages of the sixteenth and seventeenth centuries, one of which is even dated, and its church on a mound at a twist in the road as it wriggles through.

It is only a short step from Letcombe Regis to Wantage, but that can wait until the end of the chapter because the part of the Vale north of the Ock still needs to be explored.

Back to Faringdon, then, for the Wantage road, the A417, out of it, past Castle Mound where the battlements of Lord Berners' tower peep over the tops of Poet Laureate Pye's pine trees, to a side lane by Bowling Green Farm. After initial confusion about which way the path goes after passing a big Victorian house called Stanford Place, it settles into a well-marked track which takes care of itself for a good and very pleasant three miles across attractive and almost totally uninhabited country. Near Stanford Place it passes the grounds of Wadley House, the home of the Untons, but the present house would certainly not have been Sir Henry's home. The track, passing across fields and through cool woods, runs parallel to the A420 Oxford road, and only half a mile from it, but it is only occasionally either audible or visible. After crossing the lane from Buckland it goes on to Pusey.

Pusey as a village seems to exist for its big house: it has existed in its own right since Anglo-Saxon times (its name means 'pea island') and there is a vague and somewhat suspicious story of the manor being held by 'cornage': King Knut is said to have given an ox-horn to one William Pecote of Pusey as a warrant to hold his manor. A family called Pusey held it for a very long time, although by the end of the eighteenth century there were so many inheritances through the female line that the name Pusey became hyphenated with each successive new one. The house is a grand stone mansion of 1753 with lawns down to the lane and majestic trees all around; the village, along a dead-end lane, is also mainly in stone. There is in the farmyard a little black weatherboarded shed on mushroom-shaped stone stilts, a grain-store: there are quite a number of these in Berkshire still, rare in many places nowadays. That there were many more at one time is attested by the number of the mushroom-shaped supports which are used as markers for the drive-ways and entrances of modern houses. There is one of the granaries attached to the mill at Letcombe Regis, converted into a residence with the bottom bricked in around the stilts. The idea of the supports was, of course, to allow air to circulate under the floor to prevent dampness from affecting the stored grain.

The church in Pusey was built for one of the Pusey family in 1745-1750. It is a lovely little classical building with a Venetian window pattern repeated inside with arcades in the same fashion leading to the transepts. There are some elaborate memorials in the transepts, several to the Pusey family and its hyphenated heirs, and the portrait and surplice of the most celebrated member, Dr Edward Bouverie-Pusey.

Pusey (as he is usually named) took a good first-class classical honours degree from Christ Church, Oxford, in 1822. At Oxford he came into contact with Keble and John Newman and became deeply interested in theology. In 1829 he was appointed Regius Professor of Hebrew at Oxford, which necessitated his ordination: he was therefore firstly an academic, and secondly an ecclesiastic, but as time went on he became more and more concerned with the country's spiritual condition, especially after the Liberals' Reform Act of 1832. There was profound public ignorance of theological doctrine (was?) and a danger of decline through apathetic misconception of the facts. He felt that a full statement was needed of the points on which the Church of England differed from the various nonconformist sects. In 1833 he, Newman and Keble began to publish 'Tracts for the Times' which sparked off controversy and brought theological matters into discussion once more. This was the so-called Oxford Movement: Pusey's adherence to it added weight. 'He was able', Newman wrote, 'to give a name, a power, and a personality to what was without him a sort of mob.'

Newman decided eventually to become a Roman Catholic, but Pusey remained at Oxford, insisting that church doctrines be based on those of the early Fathers, like St Augustine, and the early Anglican theologians, like Hooker. Others, like Dr Illingworth of Longworth, were to continue this searching for clarification and purpose in Church teaching, a process needed from time to time.

Pusey, the village, is on the lower slopes of the Ridge; Hatford, a mile and a half away, is in the Vale, by a currently dry stream which in wetter times feeds the Ock. It was at Hatford that Sir Edward Unton married the widow of the decapitated Earl of Warwick, and St George's Church, where this ceremony took place, was until recently a ruin: a new and rather unattractive Victorian substitute was built, but now the old one, a simple nave and chancel of late Norman (mid-twelfth-century) origin, is repaired and back in service. Opposite the Victorian church is a row of cottages, in stone with a steep slated roof, plain but good-looking, said to be by the Victorian architect Street; if so, it is a rare instance of interest in so humble a project as village cottages, although Street has to his credit several schools in Berkshire villages as well as churches and restoration work.

A footpath beside the dried-up brook crosses the meadows to the large and spacious Stanford in the Vale, which has several open green spaces, tall, bleak, brick eighteenth-century Stanford House and several stone cottages: overall, an attractive variety of stone, brick, timber, thatch, tile and stone-slate. The church, behind one of the greens, was there in the late twelfth century but has been altered in most of the other church-building eras, and now has, like Coleshill, a nave roof that is almost invisible behind the crenellated Perpendicular clerestory. On the southern lane out to the main road is Penstone's Farmhouse, which presents a stuccoed front of three storeys and a partial replacement of windows, the right-hand ones being left with their seventeenth-century drip-stones.

The main road is the A417 to Wantage again, and it soon crosses the meagre Ock at Mill Farm; a mile further on there is a turning to Goosey, 'goose island', whose cottages and farmsteads are scattered about the verge of a huge green. In fact, this is another shrunken village, and as at Eaton Hastings there are on the green some very odd-looking humps and shapes which might bear investigation. The inn at the north-eastern end of the green is called 'The Pound', recalling the enclosure for stray animals which once decorated its frontage.

An astonishing number of the fields around Goosey, towards Denchworth and Charney Bassett, are covered in regular undulations, inexplicable unless they are the remains of the old mediaeval strip system. This is fairly well known, but briefly, rural settlements throughout the middle ages were usually adjacent to three or four huge open fields, crops in which were rotated year by year, always with one lying fallow with no crop, to regain its fertility. The fields were divided up among the villagers or villeins, some being retained by the lord of the manor, who held the whole manor in 'fee' to some tenant-in-chief, a noble landowner or a monastery, who in turn held it from the King. The strips were all a furlong in length ('furrow-long'), 220 yards, and eight or nine yards wide. As time went on, ditches appeared between them where each strip-holder walked to his holding, so the undulating appearance of the fields took shape. In some places, where sheep-raising for the wool-trade began to assume great importance commercially, the strips disappeared long before the close of the middle ages; others went when the monastery land was sold off in the mid-sixteenth century. In many places, however, the strip system remained, by this time not feudally maintained but rented from some smaller landowner (often the squire, lineal descendant of the lord of the manor) until the late eighteenth century. By this time the efficacy of Tull's seed-drill and Townshend's turnips had begun to sink into the conservative mentality of English countrymen, and a tremendous rush took place to enclose all remaining open fields.

Even if these at Goosey were among the last to be enclosed, it is remarkable that, after 200 years, the strip markings should still be so easily identifiable.

A visit to Denchworth, a mile or so east of Goosey, at around three o'clock on a warm, sunny afternoon in August, is liable to give an impression like that gained from a village in southern France at about the same time: one dare hardly cough for fear of disturbing the corporate slumber. There is no-one about, the inn (a white-painted stone house with a thatch) is of course closed, even the dogs cannot be bothered to bark, and the church is locked. This last is a pity, because there is inside (it is a mediaeval church well restored in 1852 by Street) a curiosity, in the shape of a brass commemorating

William Hyde, his wife and their children (numbered as the sands of the sea-shore) of 1557. It is a palimpsest, which means that the Hyde memorial was inscribed on the back of an earlier brass, discovered during Street's restoration operations, which said that King Edward III had caused it to be made on the occasion of the siege and conquest of Berwick, in the year 1333, at the request of Sir William Montague, '*foundeur de ceste mesoun*'. The '*mesoun*' (*maison*) in question was the priory of Augustine canons at Bisham, founded by William Montague, Earl of Salisbury, on the site of a preceptory of the recently suppressed Templars. Why the brass was re-used by the Hydes appears to be a mystery.

The old manor-house of the Hydes is not structurally the same as the building which occupies the site now, because that is of the late seventeenth century. But it does have one ground-floor window on the right with an ogee pointed mullion, apparently fifteenth-century, which might be a survivor of the house in which Robert Dudley's unfortunate wife Amy stayed. At present the house has a smooth white front, a neat gravelled drive, and an arched gatehouse. At the road junction near the manor-house there is the stump of a cross, a 'chipping' or market cross probably.

There are any number of fields between Denchworth and Charney Bassett showing strip-markings, to add interest to an otherwise pleasant but undistinguished series of level lanes. The name of Charney Bassett looks like a clear case of the usual combined Saxon and Norman elements, particularly as Letcombe Bassett provides another apparent instance of the second. This is not the case, however. An alternative early name for the River Ock was Charn or Cern (958) and the Domesday Book version, Cernei, means island, or place, on the Charn. According to the Victoria County History, the second element comes not from a member of the Bassett family, but from the name, Basses, of a copyhold tenement (holding) in the village. In any case, there is in the village, next to the church, an extremely interesting relic of its mediaeval manor-house, the late thirteenth-century solar wing of the hall, the private apartment of the lord and his family. It is attached to a good stone house of the last century which is currently a Quaker meeting-place.

The small church, close by the Ock, which here is shallow but smooth-running and clear, and a farmstead, has a very good Norman south door with a frieze of faces, of men and cats, and on the left of the chancel there is a little Norman doorway with a tympanum showing, in relief, a man with each hand on the neck of, and being bitten by, two gryphons. A little slip passage leads from the archway to the north aisle. Charney Bassett, bigger than Denchworth, still gives an impression of deep rustic somnolence, surrounded by woods and fields, and populated by horses, cows and chickens. Before the settlement began, however, in the Iron Age, there were few other signs of life except for water-creatures, because marshland extended from the Ock to the Ridge, and near Pusey, a mile north of Charney Bassett (this tour is an admittedly tortuous one) there was a fortress on the lowest piece of firm land of the Ridge. The only access to this low-lying fort was by means of a narrow neck of land on its north-east side, by Pusey Lodge Farm: all around were streams, marsh and swamp. It is called Cherbury Camp.

Lyford is only a mile away across the Ock, smaller but similar in character to the other Vale villages. It is distinguished by a neat little close of Georgian almshouses, whose occupants must find life a good deal more restful than those of other almshouses in, say, Abingdon or Newbury: traffic here is minimal. A lane with a few cottages leads to the manor-house, a dark stone house of the early seventeenth century, its farm buildings, and the small church, with nave and chancel of the thirteenth century (lancet windows) and some upper Perpendicular windows. It is built of rubble (small stones), but the bell-turret is wooden and inside the timber scissors-brace is visible. Parts of the old Perpendicular screen are across the tower entrance.

On the way to Garford there is a farmstead called Lyford Grange, which has a timber-framed house of the late sixteenth century, with later stone wings; this is a farmhouse, but it is not the Lyford Grange where Edmund Campion the Jesuit and his two companions were captured, in 1581: that house has entirely disappeared.

Campion was one of those who, after attempting to compromise with Queen Elizabeth I's Church Settlement, found that he could not reconcile his Catholic conscience with Anglican doctrine, went to the college at Douai and became a Jesuit. He was one of the first chosen to attempt the reconversion of the English, in 1580, a period

11 The Downs near Wantage

when Catholics in England were finding life more and more difficult. At first under Elizabeth they were not persecuted, provided that they paid fines instead of going to church and remained faithful and loyal subjects, but when it became evident that Mary, Queen of Scots, in open prison in England, was willing to become the focal point for international plots for her substitution for Elizabeth as queen, and the subsequent re-admission of England to papal obedience, any Catholic was liable to be suspected of treason. The Jesuits came to separate people the Queen was trying to unite, so she warned them against their subversive teaching. Campion was eagerly sought, as the most dangerous because the most persuasive, but was only run to earth at Lyford by treachery: in fact it seems unlikely that he would have been found any other way in so remote a corner of so remote a parish. He was tortured, for information against others, but in vain; he was tried for treason and sentenced, and said, with a good deal of reason, 'In condemning us you condemn all your own ancestors, all the ancient priests, bishops and kings, all that once was the glory of England, the island of saints and the most devoted child of the see of Peter'. He was executed at Tyburn, 1 December, 1581.

The tranquillity of this rural English landscape, in the Vale of White Horse, remains relatively untouched still by the crude rush and tumble that constitutes so much of modern life; small, sleepy, unspoilt villages, elms that have so far survived the dread disease, fields that show signs even now of a past 200 years gone by, cut corn, straw in the lanes, cattle and horses, the birds of the air, simple wholesome farm smells and sweet fresh air, the sun on one's back and the old land of England at one's feet: even modern tractors, combines and balers cannot detract from the essential quality of this landscape.

West Hanney, despite a little green, a Georgian house, and a church with brasses and a tablet to a lady who died aged 124 after living in three centuries, is touched by the fringes of a town; and East Hanney more so. A footpath to Grove saves the burden of walking along a main road in the same direction, but the penalty is that, along with some more of this golden landscape, it goes past a large and pungent sewage plant. Grove is submerged beneath a flood of new estate building, and the trudge into Wantage is not exciting.

Wantage is a hill-top town at a meeting of roads, the crossing

12 Ashdown Park

place of the north-south Oxford to Hungerford road, and that going west to east from Cirencester to Reading. In Saxon times this had less significance because roads were of small importance to the settlers, but the manor was a 'King's tun', and the king, as was the custom throughout early mediaeval Europe, spent his life moving from one to another of his manors, eating his rent: money was little used, his rent was due in the form of food, the produce of the land, and it was far easier for the king to go to the food than for the food to be sent to him. That is why there are so many places which proclaim a tradition of a Saxon royal palace in the vicinity; very few have come to light because they would have been simple wooden halls, like Hrothgar's hall, Heorot, in *Beowulf.* According to the Welsh monk Asser, who wrote his 'Life of Alfred' during the latter's lifetime, 'In the year of our Lord's Incarnation 894 light rose out of darkness. Alfred King of the English was born in the royal vill which is called Wanetinge in the district called Berrocscir.' The name, *Wanetinge,* means a place with an intermittent or 'waning' stream. It was not an important place: according to Dugdale it was not even made a market town until about 150 years after the Conquest, but by his time (1819) it had four annual fairs.

The four main roads meet at the long Market Place, which has a statue of King Alfred in the middle; it is a pleasant and spacious square with a few good examples of Georgian and Victorian architecture around it, but there is very little earlier building left except for the fine big church, which dates principally from the thirteenth century, and is cruciform, with a crossing tower and a Perpendicular clerestory. In the left-hand side of the sanctuary there is a fourteenth-century tomb with effigies of Sir William Fitzwarin, lord of the manor at the time, and his wife. It is just as well that Wantage can claim to be the birthplace of the great Alfred: what more could anyone want?

FOUR

Junctions

This chapter concerns the country between the Ock on its way to Abingdon, the Thames on its way to the gap in the Downs, the Downs themselves and the A338 on its way to Wantage. The railway cuts through the middle and so does the A34, the Oxford road which joins the ancient Ickleton Street at Rowstock Corner. The old joins the new in many unexpected ways, as we shall see.

We shall begin with a stretch of never-never-land which could be lost in some timeless void, instead of a couple of miles away from an Atomic Energy Research Establishment. This is, above all, a country of contrasts.

Half a mile out of Wantage on Ickleton Street or the Icknield Way or, as it is here, the A417, there is a track which ascends Lark Hill in a dead straight line; a short way up it another strikes off at right angles going east, up to Hound Hill and down to West Lockinge. Here begins the park scenery, the hills and dales, woods and valleys and streams of Arcadia. West and East Lockinge are close, some of their cottages are timber-framed with brick and tile and are three or four hundred years old, some are brick, built in the 1860s for an estate. Down in a thickly wooded valley where a stream flows through (or should: alas for romance, in this arid year it is as dry as a bone) stands a grey-stone towered church, and across the stream-bed are the barns and buildings of a once-great house. The only remnant of this house is its orangery, a tall-windowed eighteenth-century hall in blue and red brick: the rest is gone. There is a story.

Robert Lindsay, of Balcarres, Fife, was a soldier: as a young officer in the Royal Scots Fusiliers he served in the campaign in the Crimea and took part in most of the engagements there with the Russians. He so distinguished himself both at the Alma and at Inkerman that he was awarded the Victoria Cross (a new institution then). Before he retired from the army he engaged to marry the daughter of Lord Overstone who, having no heir, proposed to settle on Lindsay his estate with Lockinge House, in return for which he altered his name by licence to Loyd-Lindsay. He retired from the army in 1859 with the rank of lieutenant-colonel, and set about the kind of duties that a landowner was expected to undertake: he represented Berkshire in Parliament, was appointed colonel-commandant of the Royal Berkshire Volunteers, and became the first chairman of the British Red Cross.

In the 1870s a series of wet summers brought bad harvests, the dearth of corn brought a flood of cheap grain in from America (there were no more corn laws to protect the British farmer) and this brought ruin to a huge section of British agriculture. Farmers struggled to pay their rents, sowed grass instead of corn, went bankrupt. For the first time in living memory, the value of land and the rents from it were at a discount: the 'Golden Age' of Victorian England came to an end. Loyd-Lindsay's tenant farmers told him that they could not farm at a profit, he would have to lower their rents. Instead he bought them out, and created out of their holdings a vast home farm of around 7,000 acres, and by giving it capital, intelligence, energy and up-to-date methods, he ran it at a profit. At a time when, all over the country, farm-workers were losing their jobs and moving into the cities, Loyd-Lindsay's estate houses were all occupied, his staff paid, his barns full. He even built a reservoir in the Downs, and supplied water to the whole neighbourhood. He bred Shire horses and cattle, and became respected as a leading agriculturalist. In 1885 he was created Baron Wantage of Lockinge, and remained in command of his estates until his death in 1901.

Lord and Lady Wantage had no children: death duties broke up the estate and diminished its working population. At its height, estate workers occupied 180 houses in East and West Lockinge and Ardington, the village to the north nearer the A417 road: now only 60 house people actually employed on the parts of the estate (at least two racing stud farms), in the rest are pensioners or workers elsewhere. The present owner, Mr Christopher Loyd, wishing to preserve the character of the community, contacted the Council for Small Industries in Rural Areas, who interviewed applicants for useful occupation of some of the old Home Farm buildings in Ardington. According to the *Daily Telegraph* of 20 May 1976, there are potters in the old dairy, a furniture-joiner in the watermill, an upholsterer in the wash-house, and a chair-maker and rush-seat maker in another old outhouse. Social activities are on the increase and there is space for more craft-workers. Lord Wantage, one feels, would approve.

Betterton, a manor adjoining, was added to the Lockinge estate when the last of the Collins family, who had held it for at least 400 years, died. It is a basically sixteenth-century house, modernised, in beautifully kept gardens and as peaceful surroundings as anyone could desire. West and East Ginge are hamlets either side of the Ginge Brook which flows down to the Thames and becomes the Mill Brook at Drayton; the cottages are timber-framed or stone, mainly thatched, and so enfolded in this green, hilly, woody landscape that they seem detached entirely from any ordinary passage of time and belong only to some romantic artist's canvas or to an idealistic novelist's fond imaginings. The lane follows the Brook through this undulating unbelievable country until it passes Goldbury Hill and enters West Hendred, and the spell is broken.

The two Hendreds are too near the A417 for comfort, but East Hendred compensates by its quality. It is quite an extensive village, but in a compact quadrangle, with many connecting paths, passages and lanes but enough space left over for greens, paddocks and farms, ducks, chickens and other animals. It contains more superb examples of Berkshire vernacular architecture than any other village I have seen. There is, as there usually is, a reason for this: East Hendred's profusion of late mediaeval building is due to its importance as a centre and market for the wool-trade. The church reflects the wealth of the wool-merchants in the brasses to their memory and in the Perpendicular tower and Eyston Chapel, and the wooden screen, with rood, that stretches across both chancel and chapel entrances.

The village declined as its neighbour to the south, East Ilsley, rose, encouraged by King James I; but the church and the houses created by the wool-merchants' wealth remain: there are plenty of smaller timber-framed and stone cottages in other parts of the village, but the best are in the street that runs northward between the church and Hendred House. The row on the grassy bank on the right is dominated by a house, now a shop, with two symmetrical brick-nogged gables; on the left behind a garden wall is King's Manor, timber-framed with brick infilling and a stone-slated roof. At the end of the street, on a triangle in the middle, there is a little oblong Perpendicular chapel, in stone ashlar, with a contemporary timbered priest's house attached to it.

There are two more religious houses in this surprising place, both belonging to the Roman Catholic faith. One is a big church with an overhead passage-way, connecting it with a house on the other side of the lane, both built in 1865, and the other is the family chapel of the Eystons of Hendred House. The chapel, on the end of the south wing of the house, has two lancet windows which indicate that it was built in the thirteenth century; the house from the outside looks much later than that, with gables and square windows, but it seems that inside there is evidence of fifteenth-century construction. Possibly William Eyston, who obtained the property in 1450 when he married Isabel Stowe, rebuilt the house then, retaining only the chapel.

Despite the Reformation, Henry VIII's breach with the Church of Rome and the dangerous days when the menace of Mary Stuart's plots and tension with Spain meant that any Catholic was a potential traitor, the Eystons remained staunch to the old faith. During the time when Titus Oates's vicious fabrications were whipping up anti-Catholic hysteria, Bernard Eyston, a Franciscan friar, was lecturing on divinity in St Bonaventure's Convent at Douai. When the English nation, its religious hysteria forgotten, was being taught by Sir Robert Walpole how to make a commercial profit instead, one Eyston became a Jesuit, and several of his sisters (children of Charles Eyston the antiquary) entered convents.

A path from Hendred House going eastwards saves the discomfort of the main road and arrives just as precisely at Rowstock Corner where the Icknield Way, masquerading as the A417, crosses by means of irksome traffic lights the urgent streams of vehicles impatient to reach Oxford or Newbury yesterday.

'Fruitbearing Harwell' is still surrounded by orchards, which from early times have been its chief means of sustenance. It is a compact village, with little building outside its old confines: one needs to know its complexity of streets. There is plenty of timber-framed cottages along these streets, mostly of the box-framed type built from the gradually increasing agricultural profits of the late sixteenth and early seventeenth centuries, when a growing population was needing more food, but there are one or two examples of much earlier wooden houses. One is 'The Dell', a thatched cruck cottage: this method of construction was fairly common in areas where wood was plentiful. One looked for a tree with a branch at a certain angle, felled, trimmed and split it down the middle, and presto! One had a symmetrically sided gable. As similar a tree as possible for the other end, and there was the basis for a house, needing only stone base walls, some more for the gable ends, plenty of supporting rafters, and a thatch. When brick-making was re-introduced to England and bricks became cheaper (in Berkshire brick-making began earlier than many parts, because of the suitability of the component clay) then chimneys were possible instead of a hole in the thatch, and if a chimney was built, like a sturdy central column, an extra floor could be attached to it. So the box-framed house, with two storeys, replaced the cruck cottage, with only one. The mystery is why there are any crucks still standing today. 'The Dell' dates from about 1445.

Even so, the crucks are not the earliest domestic buildings in Harwell; that distinction belongs to the old manor-house Middle Farm. It is hard to detect, because there are later additions and alterations, and the outside is currently rough-cast, but the nucleus of the house is a fourteenth-century hall with a kingpost, truss, and four-way struts; some of the doorways survive and it is said that the service wing may be the frame of a hall of the late thirteenth century. There is attached to it a range of ancient thatched barns and sheds, and one of the barns is built with crucks.

The church, finding which is like looking for the middle of a maze, was built in the late twelfth century to replace an earlier structure, the remains of which were found west of the present tower in 1962. It has a screen, and a brass to the prolific Jennens family dated 1599, and in the tower-room a tablet recording the benefaction of Christopher

Elderfield who died in 1652 and '. . . gave lands for the purpose of purchasing, in the spring of every year, two milch cows, to be given to two of the poorest men in the parish of Harwell (burthened with families) for their sustenation'. Dugdale, writing in the period 1815-1819, comments that since most of Harwell's land was arable a poor man could not find pasture for a cow, so the trustees of the charity bought two cows in the winter, killed them, and distributed the meat among the poor. 'This', thought Dugdale, 'is a wretched substitute for what was benevolently intended by the donor.'

Six poor widows were subsequently provided for in 1715 by a lady of the Jennens or Jennings family, 'late wife of William Geering, Gent.', when she built and endowed a row of almshouses. These can be seen in the High Street, in brick, with little Flemish gables.

A field-track can take one out of Harwell and towards West Hagbourne, but it is now interrupted by a great chalky-white gash patrolled by huge-wheeled mechanical dinosaurs hammering out a new extension or replacement of the A34. This future delight complicates progress several times in the course of this chapter.

West Hagbourne is a small hamlet but contains several old timber-framed houses, including a cruck near the Manor Farm: most of them are thatched. On the northern horizon of the village the swarming housing estates of Didcot in the part which used to be North Hagbourne but is now contracted to Northbourne, loom darkly with a glittering top-dressing of television aerials. Instead of contemplating these one can turn to look at the stump of a market cross by the wayside where three roads meet at Coscote (Cross-cot); nearby is a seventeenth-century timbered house with decorated barge-boards (the wooden gable-eaves) and moss on the roof-tiles, called Coscote Manor. The lane then approaches the big embankment of the dead railway that used to run from Didcot to Newbury, and dives under the old bridge to East Hagbourne. Another cross, complete on steps, stands in the centre of a little square surrounded by early seventeenth-century timber-framed houses; the church is up a lane to the west of the cross, mainly thirteenth-century with a Perpendicular clerestory and east window. The north aisle and arcade are Decorated, of the fourteenth century (octagonal columns) and there is even some original bright red and blue glass in the north aisle windows. It is a good old church, very little spoiled by heavy-handed restoration, and has a notice telling of the Sanctuary anciently available within it, pointing to the Sanctuary knocker on the door.

There are many other old timbered houses in the street of East Hagbourne and at the eastern end the stump of the third market cross. 'An annual fair', says Dugdale, 'is holden here, on the Thursday before the 11th of October.'

The countryside here is a maze of watercourses from the Downs, heading towards the Thames, and is therefore flattish. The lane crosses one of the brooks by the white weatherboarded Hagbourne Mill, and from here there are good views of Blewburton Hill, an Iron Age hill-fort which is multivallate (more than one set of walls and ditches) but only on the south-western side: either it fits in with the fore-mentioned theory of defence by one Celtic tribe against another in possession of the Downs, since the fortified side faces them, or it was simply never finished.

Blewbury is even more complicated, and more compact, than Harwell. It is all crammed in an angle of the road from East Hagbourne where it meets the A417, half a mile from Blewburton Hill, and under the lee of the Downs below the outstanding wood-crested Churn Hill. The 'blew' in the title of both fort and village is from the Old English *bleo* which simply means colour, any colour. Why it should be applied to this *byrig* more than any other, whether or not the hillside is green and white where the chalk breaks through the grass, as Professor Ekwall suggests, seems to be a mystery.

It is probable that a stranger could wander around Blewbury all day, gradually going off his head, without ever finding his way to the church. Even Theseus, with or without Ariadne's assistance, would never have managed it, so intricate are Blewbury's labyrinthine ways. No doubt even the villagers occasionally get lost. Many of the houses are timbered, many are thatched, most are either well-kept or architecturally interesting, or both. Where the Minotaur sleeps, if he can be found, there is a tiny little cottage built in 1738 by one Bacon as an almshouse for the oldest inhabitant (now occupied by an elderly lady). Along from it, by the churchyard wall, is a house built and endowed by William Malthus in 1709 as a Charity School, a stylish brick house. The church is based on the late Norman building, with additions of the thirteenth and fourteenth centuries. There are some brasses, one to an early vicar dated 1496, and the fifteenth-century door to the rood-loft stairs is still in place. Outside the north wall there are two recumbent effigies on a table-tomb, badly eroded.

If a closer look at the ramparts of Blewburton is wanted, there is a field track from Blewbury which leads straight up to it; the fort is early, from about 300 B.C., and contained within its palisades a village of small, circular, timber houses, with pits for grain storage. Its pre-Belgic date does not explain the absence of defences on the north-eastern side, nor does it disprove the theory of opposition to a Downs-based tribe: having been created, the fort could be used by any subsequent defenders, and in fact evidently came into use a good deal later, since Roman-type pottery has been found there.

On the far side of the hill the path descends abruptly to Aston Upthorpe. This parish, and that of its near neighbour, Aston Tirrold, are contiguous and probably were originally one, but divided into two manors. In 964 they appear simply as Eastun, the eastern tun, but in 1316 we have 'Aston et Upthrop' and in 1380, 'Aston Turald', with the information that in the twelfth century it had been held by Nicholas, son of Turald (a Norman name of Scandinavian origin – as the Normans were). So the two manors developed separately, each with its own church. Upthorpe's is very small, a simple Norman nave with a Victorian chancel and bell-turret with a little spire, and a seventeenth-century porch. Opposite the church is a timbered house called The Smithy, which it no doubt used to be. The parish boundary runs down the middle of the central road: on the Tirrold side of it there is a neat little United Reformed Church, ex-Presbyterian, of 1728, with two Romanesque windows in each wall except the rear, which has a rose of stained glass. Footpaths cut across the lanes to the church, which has a big flint tower: the large quoin-stones could be Anglo-Saxon work, and if so then this is the original parish church, and Upthorpe was built when the parish divided in Norman times. In the porch there is some of the Perpendicular arcading from the old screen (due to sixteenth-century rural thrift, 'waste not, want not'?). There are several timber-framed cottages in the village, and some biggish Georgian houses too.

Northward from the Astons the country is flat, a broad level plain with a huge skyscape, and at ground level views of the Oxfordshire hills on the far side of the Thames. South Moreton is spread either side of its main street, having its share of the local timbered and thatched cottages, and one big Georgian house. Another great embankment blots out the landscape like a rampart across the way to Cholsey, this time bearing the main line, very much alive, to Didcot and the West.

Towards the Downs, several small hills stand out, often with clumps of trees on their crests: Churn Hill is still distinguishable from here for that reason. Just beyond the roofs and church tower of Cholsey is a hill-top without such a clump, and that is Silsbury, another Iron Age fort whose defences have been entirely ploughed out. Its position, outstanding from the Downs, would have been crucial for keeping an eye on the river approaches.

Cholsey today is not very exciting, but it once had a monastery, founded by King Ethelred II the Redeless in 986, and its church might well be the abbey church, since it is cruciform and the crossing tower, like Aston Tirrold's, has stone quoins that could be Anglo-Saxon. The manor farm was reckoned to be the biggest and best in England, with a rent of £1,000 a year, and before the Dissolution it belonged to the Abbey of Reading. For storing the tithes from this lucrative farm the Abbot caused to be built, possibly as early as the late twelfth century, a barn which was twice as big as the barn of Great Coxwell: it was demolished in 1815, but was still standing when Dugdale wrote:

> 'It measures 303 feet in length, 62 in height, and 54 in breadth. The roof is supported by 17 pillars on each side. They are four yards in circumference and in the centre rise to a great height, but next the walls are not more than eight feet high. Near one of the doors a tablet records the following:- "In this barn John Lanesley threshed, for Mr Joseph Hopkins, 5 quarters, 7 bushels and a half of wheat in 13 hours on March 15, 1747." This man continued in the same farm, receiving full wages as a labourer in husbandry, till the winter of 1804 when, in his 93rd year, he became dependent on the parish.'

The materials of the great barn were re-used for new farm buildings, and these today are on a generous scale, full of baled straw.

Cholsey has moved well away from its church and manor farm in order to be nearer the railway station and the A329 road that runs along the riverside to Reading. A long straight lane from its northern marches takes one a respectable distance from that road and only joins it half a mile from Wallingford.

It is quite clear from walking about Wallingford, let alone studying a map of it, that it is basically a planned town. It is rectangular, with important roads crossing at right angles in the middle, and it even has ramparts all the way round. They are most plainly visible from the open green space in the north-western quarter because they form its perimeter, also, more worn down, in the south-western. The castle, what is left of it, occupies the north-eastern quarter. There are very few instances of town planning in mediaeval England; one of the first is Salisbury, in the early thirteenth century, then there are the castle-towns of Edward I in the later years of that century. But the castle at Wallingford, so important to the control of the Thames valley, was one of the first stone Norman castles, playing a vital part in the civil war between Stephen and Matilda; furthermore, the earthen ramparts which quadrilaterally envelop the town are said to have been the work of early Anglo-Saxon settlers, who are not notable for having planned anything at all. It is known, however, that throughout the Roman occupation, from the 1st to the 4th century, there was a settlement in the vicinity, and that it was based on an early marching-camp of the Roman army. Could it be that the Saxon settlers found the Romano-British town habitable and threw up their ramparts around the existing perimeter?

There is very little left of the Norman castle except the steep motte, with a few broken fragments of wall, for which we have to thank the Parliamentary soldiers (or rather, those of the Commonwealth) who in 1653 were sent to demolish it. Governor Blagge had been obliged to surrender it, after a long siege at the end of the Civil War, and Cromwell evidently wished to ensure that no-one else would hold it against him. It is difficult to picture it, so little remains, but Camden helps, because he says that 'its size and magnificence used to strike me with amazement, when I came thither a lad from Oxford: it being a retreat for the students of the church. It is environed with a double wall and a double ditch, and in the middle, on a high artificial mount, stands the citadel; in the ascent to which, by steps, I have seen a well of immense depth.'

There are quantities of late mediaeval timbered buildings in the laid-out streets, and still more handsome Georgian houses in brick. In the Market Place, in the town's centre south of the crossing of the main roads, there is the Town Hall, a fine late seventeenth-century hall, half supported on pillars, with a big Venetian window overlooking the square. Behind it the parish church (one of three), St Mary's, is mostly nineteenth-century restoration work, except for the Perpendicular tower. The bridge is of stone and crosses the river in six arches, then needs another eleven to cross the flat flood-plain on the far side.

The A4130 road to Didcot is the one to take out of Wallingford for an exploration of the country north of the railway and south of Abingdon. There are first the Wallingford suburbs to be traversed and then an open field and the turning to the joint parishes of Sotwell-cum-Brightwell. Sotwell is first from this direction, with its own little Victorian church, a barn behind a Georgian farmhouse which looks as if it could have been there a hundred years longer than the farm-house, and in the village street opposite the church an extremely odd-shaped timber-framed, thatched cottage called The Small House.

Brightwell church, St Agatha's, was originally late Norman but has additions from all the subsequent ages, including a late Georgian (1797) tower in brick. North of the church is a stone house, mostly Victorian, but with a seventeenth-century wing, in a position to suggest that it might have been the rectory. The manor-house is south of the church, a big three-storey, five-bay Georgian house in blue and red brick. The name Brightwell, seems to have meant exactly what it says: in 854 it is written *Brihtanwylle,* which means 'bright spring' and at another time it was, in Latin, the manor '*ad declaratam fontem*'.

North of Brightwell there is a range of hills bordering the Thames, the penultimate of which (looking northward) is strongly fortified: it is one of two features which dominate this region, the other being somewhat more recent. Six huge cooling-towers and a towering chimney belonging to the power station at Didcot can be seen for miles around. Turning away from both a lane winds flatly to North Moreton, a pretty village with several thatched and timber-framed houses, one of which (in fact tiled, not thatched) has a hall with two gabled wings, one with an oriel window. It is called Cobb's Cottage. The church is late Norman: the south arcade has pointed arches and round pillars. The south chapel was added in the fourteenth century and its east window, a big tall one, has some of the best original glass in Berkshire, showing some of the saints and their sticky ends. According to Dugdale, the parish register for May 1598 shows a record of early football hooliganism quite in keeping with modern trends: 'John and Richard Gregorie. These two men were killed by old Gunter. Gunter's sons and the Gregories fell together by the ears at football. Old Gunter drew his dagger and broke both their heads, and they died both within a fortnight after.'

A very straight section of road from North Moreton crosses the A4130 and begins the ascent of the Sinodun Hills. It doubles back twice and then skirts the hill close to the lowest ramparts of the fort on Castle Hill. This is an early Iron Age contour fort, roughly contemporary with Uffington Castle above the White Horse. Its position, commanding both the river-plains as far as the Downs (Blewburton is plainly visible and therefore could be signalled) and the Thames as well, is obviously important militarily and it is no surprise that there are signs of Roman occupation there as well; in fact the Romans, after the initial onslaught and the fierce rebellion of the Iceni in 60 A.D. quickly civilised the south-eastern Britons and thereafter, until the piratical invasions began in the late 3rd century, had no need of military defences in the south-east, so probably the building on Sinodun was religious or civil. In the middle ages Wallingford, further downstream and nearer the gap in the Downs, replaced it as a stronghold.

The end hill, called Wittenham Clumps because of the copse on its rounded summit, overlooks a plain where the Thames meanders in a wide loop: on one side of the loop, the eastern, is Little Wittenham, on the western bend, Long Wittenham. The lesser village used to be Abbot's Wittenham because the manor belonged to Abingdon

Abbey. Its church, near the river, is mainly a Victorian rebuilding of 1863 but the tower is Decorated, with a Perpendicular top part. In the tower-room, moved there from a demolished family chapel, are memorials to the Dunch family, whose claim to fame is precarious; its members moved on the fringes of politics in the sixteenth and seventeenth centuries. The most impressive monument, of marble and alabaster, with reclining effigies and seven kneeling children below them, is to the least memorable Dunch, Sir William, whose wife Mary was an aunt of Oliver Cromwell's. Their son Edmund supported Cromwell, was made by him governor of Wallingford Castle (before or after he destroyed it is not clear) and created Baron Burnel of East Wittenham in 1658 (just in time). The Royalists, perhaps spitefully, said that Cromwell had given him 'a patent to be lord of the Lord knows what and how little he deserves it.' Another Dunch supported the so-called 'Glorious Revolution' which ousted James II in 1688 (although his wife was half-sister to James's illegitimate children), was a rather unsuccessful gambler and was otherwise unmemorable.

A long lane crosses the flat river-plain and comes in a mile to Long Wittenham which, as its name indicates, is ranged the length of a long street. This is another of those riverside sites favoured by successive communities since the very earliest times: in the neighbouring West Field (quite possibly the river bank at that time) evidence of Old Stone Age, early, middle and late Bronze Age occupation has turned up, and there was quite an important early Iron Age settlement of the kind named after La Tène, in eastern France. The present village was established in Saxon times (there was a cemetery of theirs nearby) and the church is mainly Norman, as can be seen from the chancel arch and a chancel north window. There is also a lead font which is late Norman, with a design of bishops or abbots and sun-wheel symbols. It has a very aged timber porch with a little wooden balustrade each side and seems about ready to topple over at any minute. In the south transept, which is the vestry, there is a thirteenth-century piscina with the figure of a knight on it, sitting cross-legged.

The church is at the end of a short lane, either side of which are the buildings of Church Farm, on the right the fifteenth-century timber-framed farmhouse with a jetty, on the left a thatched barn of about 1550. On the road, close by the barn, there is a derelict-looking cruck cottage, cased in brick, which is opened at the back and used as a tractor-shed. Where the road turns off at the end of the street there is a market cross, and near it an L-shaped cruck cottage (called just that) with a thatch and a perilous tilt. At the very end, past the cross and the turning, there is a house which used to be a Youth Hostel. Twenty years ago when I spent a night in it, the warden showed me and the two or three other overnight hostellers a shed in the garden where he was setting up scale models of typical Berkshire cottages as they were in the 1930s, before they were overtaken by the age of the motor-car, television and supermarket. The models, supplemented by engines and rolling stock of the Great Western Railway, were accurate to the last detail: each pane of the lattice windows was glazed, each brick was weathered to a different shade, the thatch was laid with human hair from the barber's shop floor. 'One day', the warden told us, 'I want to make these few models the nucleus of a big lay-out, to preserve a countryside as it was in the last days before everything started to change.'

Now the shed in the garden of the former Hostel is replaced by a large modern barn, the yard is full of railway signs and signals, and the Pendon Museum, housed in the barn, contains not only Roy England's (the ex-warden) models but numerous additions, and trains and a railway lay-out to please any enthusiast. The Pendon Trust is carrying on Mr England's work, over which he still presides, and its team of modellers, with still a formidable task in front of them, is continuing his precise and exacting work. It is a notably worthwhile project, carried out with a degree of excellence rare in this makeshift age.

The way from Long Wittenham to Didcot, with the massive cooling-towers looming ever closer, is not world-famous for its scenic beauty, and Didcot is not a charming old-world town full of memorable architectural pleasures. It grew, with no attempt made to render the growth easy on the eye, when the Great Western Railway magnates decided to make Didcot their junction depot. Without doubt the eponymous Dudda would not be best pleased to see how his cot has developed.

13 The River Lambourn near Weston

The original Didcot, in fact, still exists as a recognisable village around its church, and has even managed to retain a cruck cottage near it. It is also possible for a pedestrian to escape from it and reach Sutton Courtenay with reasonable despatch, considering the circuitous nature of all the roads to it from Didcot. There is a footpath which, taken at the power-station entrance, skirts its perimeter and arrives among the housing at the end of the village. No-one else appears to use it except the rabbits who are unperturbed at its hissings and roarings and effusions of steam.

Sutton Courtenay, the 'Southern tun' granted by Henry II to Reginald de Curtenai, ancestor of the later Earls of Devon, in 1161, is a slightly frustrating place because it has too many trees. The Courtenay manor-house, which must have been built within about 30 years of Henry II's grant, is fortunately near the road, opposite the George inn, and from its materials and style one can see that the incumbent Courtenay built the church tower at the same time. The hall has later windows on the south side but keeps its round-headed characteristic doorway: it has a range of modern buildings to complete the house on the north side.

But the newer manor-house, built south of the hall about a hundred years after the hall, with later additions, and its ancient barn, cannot be seen because of the trees, and neither can the Abbey, south of the church, which was not an abbey but a grange of Abingdon Abbey (that is, a residence for visiting monks while rents were collected from the manors belonging to the Abbey). It is still mainly a genuine survival from the fourteenth century. Probably the best time for an ordinary interested passer-by to catch a glimpse of these places would be in the winter, when the trees are bare.

There is a pleasant wide street, with grass verges, between these mediaeval buildings and the river, where there used to be wharves for the loading and unloading of all manner of farm produce into barges to be taken to London: Sutton Courtenay was the riverside port for all the villages of the Vale until the railway came. Beyond the 'Abbey' walls, moving southwards, there is a second section of the village, with many pleasing old cottages and houses, then the fore-mentioned housing connected with the power-station and at last an open flat road through the fields to Milton.

14 St Nicholas' Church, Newbury

Since Milton is concerned partly with the power-station and partly with the railway it is best to creep along a footpath by its northern limits, whence the church, a Victorian restoration of 1850, can be visited and Milton House seen: this is a great impressive brick house of the William and Mary era with a broad front of five bays and a tall three storeys, and later eighteenth-century wings. High brick walls surround its grounds.

The footpath continues to the Mill Brook, which was encountered earlier as the Ginge Brook, and then gets entangled with the new motorway extension also previously crossed near Harwell. The path picks up some stone metalling in its surface, which is noteworthy because it is part of the famous Causeway of Steventon, a paved way raised above ground level because of recurrent flooding of the Brook, which can still be traced from the Mill to the church. The path emerges at Milton Lane, by an excellent L-shaped timbered house called Green Farm House, thatched and recently renovated, with some of the old wooden windows replaced. Unfortunately for Steventon, the A34 runs right through it, hence the motorway extension under construction. The road bridges the railway near the vanished station: the stone cottages in the Tudor style close by, built in 1840, are still standing, however. Because Steventon was exactly halfway between London and Bristol the board meetings of the Great Western Railway used to take place there, and the cottages were built for that purpose.

A footpath on the southern side of the railway finds its way to the Brook, the Green, the church and the beginning of the Causeway. The church, mostly early fourteenth-century, is not outstanding, but the row of houses and cottages on the south side of the Causeway is a wonderful assembly of late mediaeval domestic architecture. There was a priory at Steventon, a cell of the Benedictine Abbey of Bec in Normandy. Since it was subject to an abbey in France it was declared alien by Edward III during the Hundred Years War, and suppressed. The house called Priory Cottage, at the beginning of the Causeway nearest to the church, is not likely to have existed before the priory's extinction, since the earliest part dates from the late fourteenth century, but possibly stands on the site. Other parts of the house are later additions, making a large and rambling house. It would be tedious to enumerate all the excellent examples of timber-framed houses along the Causeway, continuing beyond the break made where the railway crosses it, but at least six are outstanding and worth more than a glance. The Causeway is raised quite high and lined on both sides with trees, and crosses the A34 to continue via Milton Lane to the Mill, as mentioned.

In order to go to Drayton from Steventon there is unfortunately no alternative to the A34, so its noisy discomforts must be endured for a mile until the new section, completed at this juncture, siphons off the traffic. The road enters Drayton at the Green, where an inn faces the war memorial, a Baptist chapel of 1834, and a Georgian Gothick house with pointed windows and a gable end, painted white, with a coloured St George killing the dragon on it. The High Street runs due east from the Green: according to James Vincent, author of *Highways and Byways in Berkshire*, faint signs still showed, in 1906, of the 'closes', the old one-acre holdings of the middle ages, which used to border this street. 'Time was', he says, 'when the holders of these closes, in severalty ploughed them and turned their beasts on to the rough moor as common pasture. Now that which was common pasture is the plough-land of one farmer, and the closes, though some of them are still held in severalty, have an almost immemorial 'skin' of grass upon them.' There are now houses and farmsteads and no discernible trace of the closes.

The church, mainly Perpendicular but bearing a few Early English traces, stands near the bottom of Church Lane: where this becomes Henleys Lane, at a bend, there is a fine big sixteenth-century manor-house behind a stone wall, called Lime Close, once owned and occupied by the aforesaid James Vincent.

From Drayton a footpath can be taken, across the new road, and across two and a half miles of flat, highly cultivated arable country, with hereabouts a great preponderance of maize. It comes to the A338 near Venn Mill on the Childrey Brook, to the Ock and to 'Noah's Ark', where Chapter One began.

FIVE

Lambourn Downs

A traveller moving southwards along the A34, passing the Atomic Research Establishment on his right and the village of Chilton on his left, may notice, half way up the slope of the Downs as he ascends, a narrow rough belt crossing the road at right angles. He can trace it, to right and left, a ragged line across the face of the Downs, as far as he can see. The Saxons called it Grim's Ditch: Grim was an ogre who became synonymous with the Devil when they became Christian. If they found any peculiarity in the landscape which did not look natural and had not been effected by themselves, they frequently ascribed it to some superhuman giant: Grimsdyke, Devil's Ditch, Devil's Highway, all may be found on the map of England. This Grim's Ditch was there even before the Romans came: it was quite possibly there before the White Horse was scored in the turf of the hillside. It was a boundary-marking ditch excavated by men of the late Bronze Age, who might well have used the Ridgeway, which runs along the crest of the hill just above it; now, it is the new county boundary, at this point, between Berkshire and the Vale of White Horse district of Oxfordshire.

So now we can turn to Berkshire proper, the rump of the county left after the top third was sliced off and given to Oxfordshire. This chapter will explore the lonely Downland between the A338, the new M4 motorway, and the county boundary with Wiltshire in the west: the Lambourn Downs.

Great Shefford is as good a place as any from which to begin, it is at a crossing of the A338 from Wantage to Hungerford and the

B4000, already used to climb from Ashbury to the Ridgeway, which descends to Lambourn and follows the Lambourn river all the way to Newbury. About a mile and a half up this valley road from Great Shefford church is East Garston, a village clustered about the river and spread up the northern hillside of the valley. The river, in this sun-baked summer, is dry here (lower down it receives more generous springs and flows copiously) and the cottages ranged along its banks, many of them timber-framed with the typical Berkshire in-filling of flint or brick, and thatched, with tiny attic windows peering out under bushy thatch eyebrow-peaks, look deprived and forlorn. A railway used to run from Lambourn to Newbury, alongside road and river: the piers of its bridges can still be seen either side of the roads which ascend the hillside. One of these runs up to the church, standing aloof from the village. It has some evidence of late Norman work (in the crossing tower and transepts) and some Decorated features, but was modernised in 1875 by means of funds from local families. On the nave side of the crossing there is a painting above the arch of the Tree of Jesse, by the artist Westlake.

Footpaths abound on these Downs, but very few roads: the last building on the only road that continues over the hill from East Garston is the old School House, now a private residence. There is not, incidentally, and never was, a West Garston: the name derives from 'Esgar's tun'. One Esgar (an old Danish name) was a tenant in Lambourn in 1066, according to Domesday Book.

The lane winds into the silent, corn-filled fields of the Downs, into a valley and up again to a ridge to serve a couple of farmsteads. This is East Garston Down, and round the edge of it there is another example of Grim's evident work, another boundary ditch, showing now as a wide terrace of turf with a sharp dip into the downward slope of the hill. It runs all along the contour of the hill. Eastbury Grange, at the bottom, is about as remote a farmstead as anyone could wish for, but as one toils up the opposite hill, called Eastbury Down, taking time to spot the two barrows just visible in a field of barley, one with a shed on it, the other just showing as a patch of rough grass among the corn, and the faint terraces on the hillside on which those Bronze Age people grew their crops, it becomes clear that the hills were a centre of population, such as it was: probably they supported about as many people as they do now.

Hyde Farm, at the top, looks remarkably civilised and is only a mile from Lambourn, so a track can be taken back into the hills, along Bockhampton Down. All the while, here, the hillsides are cultivated, thick with barley, oats and wheat, growing or cut. Trees and scrub grow on the hill-tops here, but further north the top crest of the Downs, above Childrey and Sparsholt, shows bare and hard against the sky. On the height of Bockhampton Down where four tracks meet, on the south-facing slope is the site of a building of the Roman era; possibly, in this position, a farmstead, it is admirably placed, facing the sun, overlooking the long valley down to present Eastbury Grange.

There is a wireless mast on the hill directly above Sparsholt, which can be seen from a great distance around: from this crossroads, it shows at the far end of a long straight track used for exercising race-horses. In fact from here on westwards, the Downs are used extensively for training these animals in the Sport of Kings. One never sees them in the course of an ordinary day's walk, unless it happens to start at four o'clock in the morning.

Instead of going all the way to the W.T. mast, the corner may be cut by using the county boundary which here constitutes a path that crosses the only road that traverses this section of the Downs: the one that runs between Childrey and Lambourn. It keeps to the hill-tops, so it is easy to slip down the far hillside to a valley bottom where there is a Bronze Age mausoleum called Seven Barrows. There are far more than seven, nearer 20 altogether, of the Middle Bronze Age, of the types known as bell, bowl and disc barrows, from their appearance. Nearby, on Crog Hill, there is an older burial, a long barrow of the New Stone Age which was probably once like Wayland's Smithy but is now so broken up as to be almost unrecognisable. A track runs right through the middle of it, up to a fold of the hills where there are several practice courses, all thriftily supporting corn in the middle, and no other signs of human presence whatever.

The county boundary can be followed again down a steep cleft called Whit Coombe between vast acreages of barley (if unharvested) to a crescent-shaped clump of trees called Knighton Bushes, about two miles due south of Uffington Castle and the White Horse. Still there is no human habitation, yet still there are faint marks on the hillsides of Bronze Age field-terraces. There is a peculiar enclosure here near the Bushes full of sarsens, lying about in all directions. Sarsens are boulders of sandstone, left lying on the surface by the gradual erosion of their overlying sand. There are hundreds, all over Berkshire, often used in building.

A steep track climbs from Knighton Bushes up to Weathercock Hill, and the map shows a footpath continuing even more steeply down to the valley on the other side: this is only usable when the corn has been cut, otherwise there is the county boundary again which crosses the valley road, the B4000, half a mile further down.

The dense woods on the left of this road, moving back up it northwards, are in the grounds of Ashdown Park, and it is necessary to follow the drive to its stables and cottages, and possibly to take a footpath across the rear of its precincts, for a glimpse of the very odd-looking house. It is tall and narrow, four-square like a tower, in creamy chalk blocks with brown-stone corner dressings, rising three storeys and an attic to a bell-tower with a green cupola and a golden orb capping it. Originally it stood at the centre of the forest with long straight avenues in all four directions: the windows are in five bays on all four sides.

There is an odd and unhistorical story attached to the house, to the effect that in 1665 during the time of the great plague in London, the Lord Mayor Sir William Craven rode out of London to the West, through Newbury and Lambourn to the Downs, and when he thought he was far enough away from all sources of infection, built the house, or had it built by Webb, a pupil of Inigo Jones.

There is only one reasonable certainty in this story, that the style suggests that it could well have been built in the 1660s. But, according to Pevsner, 'for Ashdown we have no date, nor an architect'. Certainly one Sir William Craven was once Lord Mayor of London, but that was in the year 1610-1611, and he died in 1618. The house was built for his son, another William, whose remarkable life spanned all but nine years of the seventeenth century (1606-1697).

A young cavalier in Jacobean England, if he wanted experience of military action, could always go and offer his services to whichever side he favoured in the apparently endless religious wars that dragged on in Germany for a period of 30 years (1618-1648). While still in his teens William Craven entered the service of Prince Maurice of Orange and his successor, Frederick Henry, and so distinguished himself that when he returned to England in 1627 he was first knighted by Charles I, then a week later created Baron Craven of Hamstead Marshall (near Newbury). The wars continued, Craven returned to them, and in the service of the Electress Elizabeth of the Palatinate (James I's daughter, whose Protestant husband Frederick, by accepting the crown of Catholic Bohemia, had sparked off the whole dispute), became a permanent member of Elizabeth's court when it was in exile in Holland. He was by this time extremely wealthy, several times helped Elizabeth financially, and also contributed to Charles I's funds during his struggle with his Parliament, for which he was declared by that victorious body in 1649 an 'offender against the Commonwealth in England'; by Act of Parliament his estates were sold in 1652. Having also supplied Charles II with funds when that august personage was in need of them (as normally seemed to be the case), he returned at the Restoration and was able to recover at least some of his estates. In 1664 he was further exalted as Viscount Craven of Uffington and also Earl of Craven. He still contributed to the Electress Elizabeth's upkeep, especially when she fell on hard times and her nephew the King did nothing to help.

Craven was generous not only with his money but with his interests: when the plague, and then the great fire struck London he exerted himself strenuously to help. He was particularly fascinated by the problems of fighting fires, and always attended in person, to give assistance and advice, whenever a fire broke out in the City. This propensity of his became so well known that the story got around that his horse knew the smell of a fire before he had wind of it himself, and would immediately turn and gallop off with him to reach the spot no matter how far away it was.

Even when he was well over 80 this energetic man went on giving assistance to the unfortunate and in fire-fighting, and took great interest in the gardens of his various estates. He never married, and when he died, so did his earldom, although some of his titles and all of his estates passed to a collateral line.

The footpath from which the house can be viewed continues

upwards to a small hill-fort of the Iron Age called Alfred's Castle. It is quite possible that somewhere around these hills the battle was fought in 871 by King Ethelred I and his brother Alfred against the Danish army. The Anglo-Saxon Chronicle says Ashdown, and specifies Wessex, and that it was four days' march from Reading. Precisely where the battle, which ended in victory for the West Saxons, took place is anyone's guess. They might well have used the little hill-fort as a camp, but they certainly did not create it.

Alfred's Castle is on the highest hill of this last valley of Berkshire, but it is not clear whether it could ever have been visible from Uffington Castle: if there was any kind of system or organisation in the construction of these hill-forts, communications would surely have been an important consideration. Today there are too many trees in the way to be sure (again, winter might be a better time to find out), but if invisibility did preclude signalling, then Professor Frere's suggestion of chaotic confusion looks very probable.

The B4000 road from Ashbury can now be followed down the valley, and at Upper Lambourn, near where the little River Lambourn rises there are so many racing stables that one feels that the equine population must heavily outnumber the human. Perhaps Foalbourn or Coltbourn might now be a more suitable name, because Lambourn means just what it says: a stream where lambs are washed. Very few sheep, and very many horses, are kept on the Lambourn Downs these days.

Lambourn, biggest of the few settlements in this wide area of Downland, is a pleasant, small town with a markedly horsey flavour. It used to be a market town for the whole area, was known as Chipping Lambourn, and in addition to the weekly market had three annual fairs. But Dugdale says that even at the time when he wrote (1815-1819) the market had declined 'of late years'. The market cross still stands, its steps and shaft genuinely mediaeval.

The town is at a crossing of two roads, the B4000 from Ashbury to Newbury, and the B4001 from Childrey to Chilton Foliat, near Hungerford. Neither of them is particularly important, which gives the town a more leisurely feeling than, for example, Faringdon, and the houses are clustered around the crossing. The church is close to it and the Market Place is exactly on it.

The church is quite big, as appropriate to a market town, late Norman from the west end to the tower crossing, and a mixture of Early English (a lancet in the north transept), Decorated (south transept) and Perpendicular (tower pinnacles, east window, south chapel with battlements). The crossing arches are unchanged from their building in the late twelfth century. There are monuments to local worthies, Westburys, Estburys, Garrards and (naturally) Fettiplaces, and alabaster tombs to Sir Thomas Essex and his wife. The village stocks, apparently now redundant (why? Surely there are plenty of likely candidates for a session in them? Why not the rowdy boys who disturb the peace with their motor-cycle engines at maximum revolutions and minimum silencing?) are pushed into a corner of the north chapel.

Close by the churchyard an embattled brick gatehouse dated 1852 leads into the Estbury Almshouses, which are apparently built on the site of yet another (possibly mythical) West Saxon royal palace. Close behind them, down a pathway, is a Wesleyan Methodist chapel of 1835, and in the churchyard wall there remains a gateway with a coat of arms over it, in stone: a seventeenth-century remnant of the vanished Lambourn Place, the manor-house.

Dugdale tells a very peculiar story, repeated with circumspection in other quarters, about certain lands in Lambourn which, he says, 'according to Blount in his "Ancient Tenures" . . . were holden by the service of keeping six "*meretrices*", alias harlots, at the King's charge. The service of taking care of the King's mistresses was not uncommon in the days of feudal tyranny'. Maybe, but dubious, to say the least, considering the tremendous influence born by the Church during the middle ages in matters both ecclesiastical and secular. All things were known to the Church: the very clerk who would write down such a service would of necessity (since no-one else but churchmen could write 'in the days of feudal tyranny') be a priest. It is a racing certainty (an expression apt enough for Lambourn) that no mediaeval churchman would condone such a service in feudal law. What may have happened is a mistake in transliteration: some copy-clerk, his mind inattentive, may have written '*meretrices*' instead perhaps of '*mercennarii*' (servants) or possibly '*meritorii*' (lodgings).

Following the road and the course of the dried up Lambourn

stream the last houses of Lambourn are left behind and at a sudden bend there is Bockhampton Farm, whose farmhouse has a mediaeval wing, of flint with mullioned windows. Eastbury is very pretty, with many thatched, timber-framed and brick or flint-filled cottages, but like East Garston it suffers somewhat from the indignity of a dried-up stream bed, like a seaside town left by the sea, or a railway town without trains (Eastbury has a dead railway too).

The valley road crosses the A338 where the two valleys meet, at Great Shefford. The village has left the vicinity of the church and manor-house, at the top of a rise on the Lambourn road, to cluster round the crossroads, where the A road wriggles to cross the sundry streams of the Lambourn (here somewhat wetter) and then climb the long hill towards Hungerford. Although there are some respectable timbered, brick and stone cottages in the village, it is the group at the top of the rise which holds the attention. Between the former rectory, a wistaria-covered Georgian house on the right, and the Manor Farm, whose house probably has a sixteenth-century nucleus, there is a narrow avenue of tall beeches leading to a Tudor-shaped brick and flint gateway extending from the wall of Manor Farm. Beyond it are church and churchyard, standing high over the green valley.

St Mary's, Great Shefford, is the only church in Berkshire which has an original round tower, probably of Norman origin. It has an octagonal top stage, but the flint of the cylinder matches the walls of the rest: the south doorway is late Norman, pointed with dog-tooth moulding, and on the east wall by their Decorated replacement, the shapes of the lower two round-headed lancets of the Norman triplet are still visible. The nave and chancel are not separated by an arch: the tower arch and the chancel lancets are Early English (thirteenth-century), so here is a simple flint church built in the late twelfth century with a few necessary replacements and embellishments in the course of time. The latest are the painted reredos and the textual mural paintings, of the last century.

Down through the village, across the shallow streams, past the Strict Methodist chapel and the place where the vanished railway used to cross the road, and on the right of it there is a field-track to the manor of East Shefford or Little Shefford. Shefford means 'Sheep ford', another indication of the time-honoured preponderance of these animals, now so seldom seen, on the Berkshire Downs.

The manor-house and the church stand together, as ever the same: it is rather like the joke about the Yeoman Warder at the Tower explaining about the headsman's axe that executed Sir Thomas More (or some other worthy), which has had a new head and a new shaft, but is still the same axe. In most cases in English country parishes, neither the church nor the manor-house is the same building as when the Saxon thegn or Norman lord erected both, but so often both still occupy the same site. In the long years following the re-introduction of Christianity to this island there was very little of the kind of centralised control over it that later developed from the eleventh-century extension of Papal authority. The man who held the manor lands built the church and appointed the priest; naturally he would build his church near his manor-house, so that his tenants, coming in from their holdings, could pay their dues to God and to himself without having to travel far from one to the other. That, briefly, is the underlying reason for the church-and-manor-house group, repeated all over the countryside of England, and it also gives a clue to some apparently diminished villages: the tenants were so far from each other in some regions (the open-field strip system was by no means universal) that there never was a village. There is no rule in these matters, a different background governs nearly every case.

The case of East Shefford is of a recently repaired church and a comparatively new manor-house, and a scattered village of a few cottages and farmhouses. The Lambourn, now a shining silver ribbon, courses through the parish alongside the road. Pevsner wrote (not long ago) that the church 'looks disused', but indicates its Norman origin by a north window, the rest Perpendicular. Monuments in it commemorate fifteenth- and sixteenth-century Fettiplaces, who then held the manor, and Dugdale says that they rebuilt the manor-house, whose 'ruins yet remain', so the present elegant house with fine gardens terraced down to the river was built since 1819, although the rear wings suggest that the earlier house was at least partly reparable.

On the top of the opposite hill there is an earthwork of Saxon origin called Hug Ditch, facing north-west, and down by the river where the old railway runs the contractors who constructed it found a Saxon cemetery: there were skeletons, which postulates a post-

Christian date, since before their conversion the Saxons tended to cremate their dead (although that practice was not universal). If Hug Ditch was a defence work, which seems possible because of its site, it may have been against possible attack from the direction of the Downs: if its date is very early, say 6th century, it might have been made by Romano-British defenders of their native land against the Germanic invaders; if contemporaneous with the cemetery, perhaps against the incursions of the pagan Mercians in the 7th or 8th century.

Just past the old mill-house at East Shefford a track leads off to the right, first to a sewage plant, then deep into the hills where, among beech-woods sheltering silent corn-fields, it loses all contact with the outside world. It soon finds it again, because over the crest of a hill it meets tracks from two farmsteads from which can be seen and heard the non-stop traffic on the M4 motorway. At this point the M4 runs roughly parallel with, and uses the same level of hillside as the Romans' Ermin Street: the track from Wickfield Farm meets this, and after a modern wiggle to negotiate the motorway it goes on to Wickham and heads steadily south-eastward. For long miles it is the basis of modern roads, but its course north of Newbury is conjectural. It crosses the Kennet below Thatcham and heads for Calleva Atrebatum, the cantonal capital in the Roman province of the subject Atrebates. Unfortunately, by reason of some county-boundary chicanery in the past, the site of this excellent example of a Romano-British town is in Hampshire, so comes outside the limits of this book, but I should like to refer to it again in a later chapter.

Wickham and the country I am about to explore are south of the M4 and therefore beyond this chapter's boundaries, but they belong more to it than to that on the River Kennet and its valley. Wickham is a small, woody hill-village with several attractive cottages and its church and manor-house on the top of its hill. Here could hardly be a better example of what I was trying to explain with reference to East Shefford: the manor-house is part Georgian and part Victorian Tudor with mullions and chimneys, and the church is all restoration work of 1845-1849, in flint ashlar, except for the lower section of the projecting south-west tower. The flints in it are bigger and rougher, laid in a crude herringbone pattern, with big stone quoins; small round-headed windows follow each other up the west wall, on the north and south walls are double-light windows with a central pillar and below this on the south side a large round-headed window, blocked. It is original Anglo-Saxon work, very rare, because pre-Conquest English builders did not often use stone.

Beyond the church a lane drops into some open undulating country with the hills of the North Hampshire Downs forming a striking horizon. Orpenham Farm, on a turning right from the lane, has a huge black thatched barn, and one of the little weatherboarded granaries on mushroom stilts. The lane winds on through silent, sun-soaked, somnolent corn country, to all appearances a thousand miles away from concrete, oil, technology and politics. It must be recorded that this kind of by-way tranquillity, encountered so many times in modern Berkshire, has been made possible largely by the much-execrated (by me too) motorways, which have had the effect of channelling all heavy and fast traffic away from these roads and lanes, returning to them something like their pre-motor-age calm.

At Hungerford Newtown, which is not all that new since several of the cottages have stood there for 300 years or more, the lane crosses the A338 and winds on into heavily wooded and apparently almost uninhabited hills, and by a series of by-ways and turnings makes its way to Membury, which is mostly in Wiltshire but by some quirk has a corner in Berkshire, so can be claimed. Membury is a large hill-fort with two sets of walls and ditches, difficult to approach because much overgrown but accessible from the north. Its inner ramparts and ditch are particularly impressive, as if dug yesterday instead of over 2,000 years ago. The wide centre (it is oval-shaped) is used, reasonably, for growing corn. A small airfield lies to the east of it, and a concrete track from it runs somewhere near the north entrance to the fort: it can be taken to its footbridge across the M4, and on to Ermin Street. A long, straight, four-mile walk along this can be enjoyed, in appreciation of the Romans' skill in picking just the right position for their road, productive of the least gradient troubles, back to the A338 again and the long hill down to Great Shefford, from which the next expedition can be mounted into the Downland of the east.

SIX

Berkshire Downs

The Downs east of the A338 are far more inhabited than those of the last chapter, which is not to say that they support a heavy-density population. There are more villages and more farmsteads, and less sense of remoteness; the A34 scythes through the middle, and the eastern side rests on the banks of the River Thames. There is more cattle, but still not many sheep; plenty of race-horses and huge acreages of corn; thick woods and a complexity of lanes, with buses and more (but not many more) cars.

From Great Shefford up the A338 valley road, at just over a mile distant a road runs off to the right steeply and directly up the hillside. At the top there is a lane to Chaddleworth, a village scattered over a triangle of lanes. The church and manor-house are at the apex: the church looks oddly elongated because in 1851 a chancel was added to the original Norman nave and chancel combined. The tower was added in the early thirteenth century, probably not very long after the rest was built, and was evidently repaired in 1637 since it has a tablet with that date high up. It also has a tiny window with wire-netting over it: I was surprised to see an owl blinking out of it at me, no doubt equally surprised.

Chaddleworth House is an early nineteenth-century replacement for the earlier manor-house, a fine classical building of 1830 or thereabouts with a Tuscan porch (a plain flat canopy with free-standing pillars). There is a hair-raising custom, related by the interesting Dugdale, concerning the recovery of 'free-bench' (right to her husband's property) by incontinent widows, but as it also prevailed at Enborne, near Newbury, it can wait until the next chapter.

On the bottom of the three roads (physically: the church is on the top of the hill) there may be heard sounds indicating the near presence of a school, if it is a break period in term-time. It is not the same school, and there are certainly more children, but in 1720 a Mr William Saunders founded one in Chaddleworth for the education of eight poor children, two from Chaddleworth itself, two from Brightwalton, two from Leckhampstead and one each from Fawley and Great Shefford. Apart from the two local infants, they all had a long way to walk each day, the one from Fawley (three valleys away to the north-west) more than eight miles, there and back!

The Chaddleworth cottages are a mixture of Berkshire vernacular (timber-framed, brick in-filling and thatched roof), Georgian in brick, and modern, and so, across a couple of miles of corn-fields and woods, is Brightwalton. The lane from Chaddleworth joins another at Brightwalton Green, where on the corner by a thatched cottage are the premises, in a series of black, green-roofed huts, of a firm engagingly called H. G. Wells & Sons Ltd., Building Contractors and Funeral Furnishers. Most of the village is on a hill-top half a mile from the Green, a cluster of timbered cottages, whose brickwork has been uncharacteristically whitened, around a wholly Victorian church, school and rectory.

The further north in these Downs, the hillier the landscape becomes; Farnborough is on a high ridge, narrow and windswept, with several good cottages, a small Norman church in flint ashlar and a Perpendicular sandstone tower, and a very elegant rectory, across the way, a model of symmetry and harmony which was nevertheless built at two periods: first in 1749 the principal block in grey and red brick, then in 1800 the top storey and lantern. It has neat lawns and a protecting circle of tall trees against the wind.

From Farnborough the road swoops down towards the last trough in the Downs before the scarp ridge, along which the Ridgeway runs. In all this three-mile journey to West Ilsley there is only one habitation, a house at the bottom appropriately called Land's End. Above it, on the heights of the Downs, is a wood-clad peak called Scutchamer Knob. It has also been known as Cuckhamsley Knob,

15 The Gateway, Donnington Castle

both of them corruptions of the name of a barrow burial on the top, in the middle of which there once was a large oak stake: it may have been the 'stapol' to mark a meeting-place, because at one time it was the Shire-moot of Berkshire, the meeting-place for the dignitaries of the whole county. A tenth-century document refers to the '*gemote aet Cwicelmes hlaew*'.

This lonely road, more in character with the western Lambourn Downs, reaches West Ilsley after climbing to and descending from a considerable height. The village, which has one particularly good box-framed cottage, probably of the early seventeenth century, in Dugdale's time had two breweries, 'the beer of which is thought particularly fine'; it has none now, but faint traces remain, such as a range of brick buildings with some odd-looking arches near a row of modern houses called Morland Close (Morland is a brewer of Abingdon) and, at the end of the village, a new house called 'The Malthouse'.

More racing-stables and practice-courses announce the imminence of East Ilsley, which is reached from this direction by a tunnel under the A34. The fortunes of this village were founded on its tremendous sheep market (wrested, as we have seen, from East Hendred) and the best of its houses can be dated to the period when the market was at its height. Several eighteenth-century houses can be seen around the village, the best of them East Ilsley Hall, tall and square, fairly early, in blue and red brick, and opposite Kennet House, larger and longer, with a little scalloped porch canopy and an early Queen Anne look to it. The church is at the top of the hill, on the side of which most of the houses stand: it dates mainly from the early thirteenth century, with an arcade of three bays, and a Decorated tower. Below the hymn and psalm boards there is a brass dated 1606 to Katherine Hildeslea, all in Latin, beginning '*Defuncti defuncta iacet Hildesleia . . .*'.

In Dugdale's time the sheep market was going mightily strong: he supposes that it was then the largest in England outside London. It started on the Wednesday in Easter week every year and went on every alternate Wednesday through the summer. The sheep were bought by graziers from the Home Counties of Hertfordshire and Buckinghamshire, who took the sheep and fed them for the London market.

16 *above* The Royal Military Academy, Sandhurst; 17 *below* Bear Wood, near Wokingham

In Vincent's time (1906) the sheep sales were still of great importance, but not for much longer: refrigerated ships could bring in massive quantities of cheaper lamb and mutton from Australia and New Zealand, and that killed the market for home-bred meat. Halfway up the steep hill between the two inns at the bottom and the 'Star' at the top, there is a grassy field on one side of the road and a bank on the other, on which is a notice saying that this was where the East Ilsley Sheep Fair was held, fortnightly all the summer, and that the last one was held in 1934.

There was an alternative: William Augustus, Duke of Cumberland, second son of George II, while still in his 20s commanded the British Army in its engagements during the War of the Austrian Succession, and when it successfully defeated the rather half-baked attempt by Charles Edward Stuart to regain the crown of England and Scotland for his father (the Old Pretender). Cumberland is usually execrated for his part in the suppression of this rising: Charles, in justice, deserves far more opprobrium for having started it. The responsibility for the destruction of the last tribal society in Europe (the Gaelic highland clans) lies with the incompetent, feverish, over-ambitious prince who had failed to notice that England, fat and prosperous after Walpole's long tutelage, wanted neither him nor his drab Catholic father. After the wars, in 1748, Cumberland returned home with an interest in racing horses, founded the course and meeting at Ascot, conveniently near to Windsor Great Forest, where he lived, and built a training stable at East Ilsley. There he bred some famous horses and began a tradition which is not only very much alive today, but half the sustenance of the Berkshire Downs from Lambourn to Streatley.

Several tracks run north-eastward from East Ilsley to the bare Downs, in fact there is such a network of them up there that it is quite easy to choose the wrong one. They exist principally for the horses and the landscape is something like the scene in the Lambourn Downs without the sense of remoteness, because the horizon is rimmed with signs of human activity, from glimpses of the A34 to the hill-top buildings of an Agricultural Research Station near Compton, and northward a huge view over the 'Junction' country, Atomic Research buildings, power-station cooling-towers, railways and all.

Nearer to hand there is the tree-capped hump of Churn Hill, landmark for so far round in the north, an assortment of tumuli and other Bronze Age barrows, the lineless track of another dead railway that used to run from Didcot by an ingenious series of loops through the Downs to Newbury, and a rifle range with red flag flying and a crackle of shots. There is also a section of the Ridgeway which carries on its imperturbable way to the edge of the Downs and the river: it skirts bald-headed Lowbury Hill, a much-ploughed hill-fort, on the south side of which there is another barrow and the site of a Romano-British temple. It is a high and lonely place, typical of those chosen for pagan worship. A track forking right from the Ridgeway passes a pessimistically named farmstead, Starveall, and in a little over a mile comes to the village of Aldworth.

At the junction of the track from the Downs with the village street there is a triangle of land with a little Ebenezer Primitive Methodist chapel, dated 1864, which appears to be disused. On the other side of the road, opposite the 'Bell' inn there is a timbered, tiled cover for a well and pump. A little way down the lane to the right is the church. Dugdale records, in the churchyard, a yew tree measuring 27 feet in circumference; in Vincent's time, 100 years later, it was still 27 feet in girth; Pevsner, not long ago, records the same dimension. Now the tree, reckoned 1,000 years old, is down, split asunder, dead.

The chief glory of St Mary's Church, Aldworth, now that the yew tree is gone (and if it really was 1,000 years old it was growing when the present church building was put up) is a series of fourteenth-century stone effigies, all of the same family, nine in number, six of them under decorated canopies. They commemorate members of the family de la Beche, who had held the manor from the Conquest onwards. Their manor-house was fortified by licence from Edward III, but there is no trace of it now: the farmhouse of Beche Farm stands on or near the site.

All the effigies are defaced, broken in some way, because the church was visited in the 1650s by Puritan iconoclasts who, seeking to destroy the pleasure of others in pictures, glass and statues because they thought it impure and irreligious, by smashing these things gave vindictive pleasure to themselves. The incumbent curate, John

Longland, resigned in disgust.

The church itself, as the lancet windows in the tower show, was built in the thirteenth century or earlier, but the main body was rebuilt in the fourteenth century, probably by the de la Beche family: the big south aisle has octagonal piers with the figures of fierce dogs as hood-mould stops.

Aldworth has a number of attractive Berkshire-style cottages, ranged about the B4009 road which runs from Newbury to Streatley. The way to Streatley along it provides some fine views of the Thames Valley and the Chilterns, and the river plains, Londonwards, beyond. A thickly wooded steep hill slithers down to the important Thames valley road (important for all time: everyone who has inhabited, conquered or occupied our land has used it) and Streatley. The village of Streatley lies on either side of a street which slopes from this road down to the river, where it crosses by a bridge to Goring, immediately on the other side.

The houses in the street are substantial, brick-built, mainly of the seventeenth and eighteenth centuries: the road, an early and obvious candidate for improvement by a turnpike trust, guaranteed prosperity to a village at the entrance to the river gap so near to the junction of the roads from Oxford and from Wantage and the West. The best of the houses is Streatley House, late eighteenth-century, a great square brick house of three storeys, relieved by a pretty porch. Between the street by the bridge, and the church, down a short lane, there was a range of malthouses which, being disused, were converted cleverly by the architect Ravenscroft, in 1898, into a village hall and meeting rooms: they have a look, however, more of the conversion than of the original. The church was rebuilt in 1865 in the Early English style, with lancet windows, but the fat, square Perpendicular tower was left.

From the bridge, the river looks quite enchanting: the smooth shining water glides between moored boats, willows cascade their billowing boughs from the banks, people relax in the sunshine on the terraces of the inn. For those who, like myself, think that the gleam of water is necessary to provide that touch of argent to combine with the vert of the trees and grass, the or of the corn-fields and the azure of the sky to make the heraldic achievement of the landscape complete, the view from Streatley Bridge must give immense satisfaction.

The latter emotion is less easily come by during the walk along the busy valley road to Basildon, but it is inevitable because there is no other way to get there. The road is cut into the steep hillside and shaded by great beeches, and there are glimpses of the river and of the graceful white house on its banks called The Grotto, built in the eighteenth century by Lady Fane. The railway bridge across the river, too, is worth a glance: it is Brunel's, to carry the line from Reading to Didcot (it re-crosses the river near Moulsford); it is brick-built, with four handsome, wide Roman arches. It is as if, as Donald Maxwell suggests in his *Pilgrimage of the Thames*, he recognised the supreme importance of the gap in the Downs to the Romans' road system, so vital a part in the government of their immense empire. In fact the site of a Roman building was discovered on the Berkshire side of that same bridge.

Basildon, as might be expected, has moved away from its early site around the church and manor-house, half a mile nearer to the river, in order to cling to the potentially lucrative road traffic. To the early Saxon settlers, so parochial in their outlook, roads, as means of communication with other settlements, were of marginal interest: the river and the fertile land on its banks were far more useful.

The church has not been neglected by its fugitive villagers: in fact the earliest complete part of it is the brick tower, erected when the toll-road was already in full swing. The rest, originally thirteenth century, was heavily restored (or, more correctly, rebuilt) in 1875. On the south side of the church, outside, leaning against a buttress, there is a tablet which reads: 'To the memory of Jethro Tull, Pioneer of Mechanized Agriculture, Author of Horse-hoeing Husbandry. Baptized in this Church 30th March 1674, Buried here 9th March 1740. Placed by Child-Beale Trust 1969.' The latter trust administers the estate immediately to the south of the church, and currently runs it as an outdoor zoo.

'The sonne of Jethro and Dorothy Tull' nearly became a politician. He studied law at Gray's Inn and was called to the bar in 1699, not because he wanted to practise but with a view to fitting himself for a career in politics. But no matter how his learning may have qualified him as a legislator, his health appears to have disqualified him: soon after his marriage in October 1699, to one Susanna Smith, instead of finding a seat in Parliament he found one on one of his father's estates at Howberry, on the other side of the river from Wallingford, and began to take an interest in farming it.

This keenly intelligent man soon brought his intellect to bear on the problems of agriculture, which were principally caused by methods which had not changed greatly since Roman times: in fact in some respects Roman ideas were more progressive, for they had introduced several improvements. In England in 1700 a sower still went forth sowing, throwing handfuls of seed at each step haphazardly on the soil, and some fell by the wayside and was trodden down, and the fowls of the air devoured it, and some fell on stony ground and withered away, and some fell on thorns and was choked, and only a very small percentage fell on good ground and bore fruit a hundred-fold, and if it did the weeds grew up around it and shared the goodness of the soil. Tull determined to introduce some fresh air into the staleness of this custom, and devised a new way of sowing sainfoin, a kind of clover used as cattle-food when dried like hay. It was not the way his labourers' fathers, grandfathers and remotest antecedents had sowed sainfoin, so they would not co-operate. Tull therefore, in his own words, 'resolved to contrive an engine to plant St. Foin more faithfully than such hands would do. For that purpose I examined and compared all the mechanical ideas that ever had entered my imagination, and at last pitched on a groove, tongue and spring in the soundboard of the organ. With those a little altered and some parts of two other instruments, as foreign to the field as the organ is, added to them, I composed my machine. It was named a drill, because when farmers used to sow their beans and peas into channels or furrows by hand, they called that action, drilling'.

He also invented a horse-drawn hoe, which could move along the neat rows of plants and dig out the weeds, allowing the crop full benefit of the manured soil. These new methods brought him considerable success, but after nine years his health seems to have given way again and he moved to Prosperous Farm, near the Wiltshire border south of Hungerford, where the climate might suit him better than the misty river-valley. In 1711, still unwell, he went abroad and travelled for two or three years in France and Italy where he noticed in some parts ploughed vineyards, where instead of manuring the land they pulverised it, breaking up the earth to a fine powder, between the rows of vines. He tried it at Prosperous Farm with turnips, then wheat, added his own improvements and found that he could grow wheat in some fields for 13 years at a stretch without manuring.

During the last ten years of his life Tull published his views and experiences, but received nothing from his contemporary farmers but scorn and abuse; in addition to his normal difficulties in getting his labourers to use his machines properly he was also beset by worry about his son, a spendthrift who persisted in gambling unsuccessfully. Tull died aged 68, unrecognised as anything but a crank, and was taken to Basildon to be buried. Some time after his death his works were translated into French, and fresher minds began to notice the logic of his ideas. Even Voltaire recommended them, and by 1784 they were in general use. They necessitated enclosure of land, of course, since the machines could not operate on the old strip system, and the scramble in the 1780s to enclose was the result. Ultimately, Tull's inventive mind provided the means to feed the tremendously increasing population of the nineteenth century.

The road to Pangbourne passes on its right the hilly parkland of Basildon House, which although invisible from the road is said to be the most splendid Georgian mansion in Berkshire. It was built by John Carr for Sir Francis Sykes (who is accorded an extravagant monument, re-using a fourteenth-century canopy, outside the church) in 1776, and its style can be assessed from the entrance gates, piers and lodges on the roadside.

After crossing, with difficulty, the railway, the road accompanies it down to the riverside and there, along Shooter's Hill Road, stand a series of flamboyant, self-confident Victorian villas redolent of 'Belle Époque' boating parties, crinolines, straw hats and champagne: they are known now as the Seven Deadly Sins.

At Pangbourne the River Pang, whose course appears in more detail in the next chapter, joins the Thames. Actually the Pang itself ought to be called the Pangbourne (like the Lambourn) because that is its proper name: it is a curious derivation, the reverse of the usual naming of a place after a river. The settlement was written in 843 as '*Peginga burnan*', the stream of Pāega's people, and by the time of Domesday Book it had become, more recognisably, 'Pangeborne'. Bourn was the river, Pāega-inga the settlers, yet the river acquired the name Pang from the settlement.

The Thames at Pangbourne is the chief joy of the place, another delightful river scene with the lock and weir, the Nautical College boat-house, all the pleasure boats, the riverside inns and the picture-framing tall trees: sunshine on the water and laughter in the air. The town is less pleasurable so it is best to find a way through it on the road to Purley, turning off right on a lane that follows the course of a brook, beside the wooded grounds of Purley Hall. It goes to Sulham, which is near enough to arterial roads and railways for its excellent timber-framed cottages to have been bought and cared for by people who can afford to do it well. The brook shares a wooded vale with the Pang, and it is a surprise to see among the fields and trees, dotted here and there, some concrete gun-posts of the 1939-1945 war: their military function seems obscure.

A footpath from the lane to Tidmarsh church crosses the Pang, a cool clear stream set about with green lawns, moorhens and fish, a lazy afternoon's dream of quiet loveliness. The church has a rarity, a pentagonal apse built in the thirteenth century with the chancel. The highly decorated south door shows that it was added to a Norman building, and the timber tower and shingled spire came later still.

From Tidmarsh in the Pang vale the ascent is long and steep back into the Downs; a glimpse through the trees on the way up shows Pangbourne Nautical College, built for the purpose in the late 1890s in a William and Mary style; nearer at hand is the genuine early Georgian Bere Court. It is a long way, through thick woods and corrugated country, to Ashampstead, and not much to see when it is reached except clusters at a series of crossroads of timbered cottages. From the last of these the B4009 road can be joined again as far as the pretty village of Hampstead Norris (or Norreys, as it is also spelt). In addition to some very attractive houses and cottages, and a large church bearing work of all ages including a quoin in the nave wall which might be Saxon, there is evidence in the vicinity of earlier inhabitants. To the north there is a rather incomplete Iron Age fort,

Perborough Castle; southward there is the site of a Roman house, with occasional evidence of Romano-Britons in other parts of the parish, and in the wood immediately behind the church and the embankment of the defunct railway line there is an earthwork of unidentifiable antiquity.

The second part of its name has only been acquired since 1500, when Sir William Norris was given the manor, which adjoined his land at Yattendon, as a reward for his service to the King, Henry VII. He seems to have been rather inconsistent in his loyalties, over a long career, as probably very many men were in the political upheavals of the fifteenth century. He was knighted when a very young man for his conduct at the Battle of Northampton, on behalf of the Yorkist faction, and later became knight of the body to Edward IV. But in 1483 he joined the rebellion against Richard III of his erstwhile supporter the Duke of Buckingham, and was attainted of high treason, as well he might be. He managed to escape to Brittany, where he joined the only remaining Lancastrian claimant, the Welshman Henry Tudor, Earl of Richmond, and returned to England in his successful train. In 1487 he commanded some of the King's troops at Stoke, the last battle of the civil wars (whose outcome was frequently in great doubt: 1485 was no dawning of a new age to contemporaries, just another squalid usurpation); afterwards he received many manors as steward to the King.

The road and the old dead railway run parallel to Compton, which, surrounded though it is by signs of Roman and pre-Roman habitation, is not in itself remarkably interesting. The old railway, of which only the line-less track remains, must have been one of those branch-lines reminiscent of Messrs Will Hay and Rowland Emett, with stations, Shaw, Hermitage, Hampstead Norris, Compton and Upton, like a line from Michael Flanders' song 'The Slow Train'. It is for the preservation of such memories that the Pendon Museum was devised.

For the return journey to Great Shefford from East Ilsley, there is a cross-country expedition which should interest any devotee of footpath-finding: take the track directly opposite the entrance to the tunnel under the A34, and keep going westwards. Secret hollow ways, admittedly rather nettle-infested, take an intrepid traveller deep into quite uninhabited (save for rabbits) country and, if they fail to lose him in the woods, bring him spot-on to Catmore, which, next to Eaton Hastings, must be one of the least populous parishes in the county. There is a tiny Norman church, extensively overhauled by the early Victorians, a rambling farmhouse of uncertain age which was probably the manor-house, and a few cottages along with farm buildings, and nothing much else. For all that it is more interesting than Leckhampstead, which seems to have an oddly suburban air, inconsistent with its wholly rural situation, and although it would be helpful to see the part of Poughley Farmhouse that belonged to the priory of Augustinian canons who, no doubt, from the twelfth-century time of their foundation served many of the neighbouring parishes, it is now within the bounds of R.A.F. Welford, so out of bounds to us.

SEVEN

Kennet

Hungerford is on the south-west borders of Berkshire, on the River Kennet where it flows into the county from the Wiltshire hills. When John Rennie constructed the Kennet and Avon Canal the course had to be engineered through the old town, because the Kennet and the canal come into it from different directions. No doubt some houses had to be bought and knocked down when the canal was dug; others had to be compensated for a difference in approach, like the two either side of the canal bridge in the High Street, which were provided with iron footbridges to new front doors in the first floor, because the ground floor was now below the new road level as it climbed to the bridge. The canal brought the town great prosperity in its heyday, which, since it was an important commercial artery must have lasted throughout the nineteenth century if the Town Hall, in best Victorian Byzantine of 1870, is anything to go by. It did have three annual fairs and a weekly market, and its wide and pleasant High Street, from the canal, under the railway bridge and up to the Town Hall, is flanked by good-looking houses of all post-mediaeval ages, like No. 27, called Hungerford Arcade, a gabled, irregular building probably of the seventeenth century, and two doors away the ironmonger's which claims to have been in 1558 the Greyhound Inn.

There is a bit of a mystery about the origins of the town's name: Vincent, in *Highways and Byways in Berkshire*, says that it is 'named after the Hungerfords, the original holders of the manor', and Dugdale says that it was known as 'Inglefol' or Ingleford at the time of Domesday Book. But the manor, belonging for some years to the Duchy of Lancaster, was granted by Henry IV to Sir Walter de Hungerford, a firm supporter, while he was still Duke of Lancaster (therefore not later than 1399); yet Ekwall finds the town's name as 'Hungreford' as early as 1101! An earlier Hungerford had given land to Hungerford church and was buried there in 1355, so perhaps the family, although apparently seated in Heytesbury, Wiltshire, since the twelfth century, moved there from the manor of Hungerford, and then recovered the latter through Sir Walter's Lancastrian service.

Unlike the Dunches of Little Wittenham, a long line of successive Hungerfords were into every political turmoil in English history, up to their necks (a not inapt expression since several of them suffered mortal injury to that part of their anatomy). Another book would be necessary to tell the story in full, but here is a brief review of the family's activities over 300 years or so.

First, Sir Thomas, a nephew of the Robert who was buried in Hungerford church in 1355, because he was a strong supporter of John of Gaunt, Duke of Lancaster, became, as successor to Sir Peter de la Mare the first named Speaker of the House of Commons (Sir Peter was certainly Speaker, but had no recognised office as such). His son Sir Walter, continuing the Lancastrian connection, was given the Hungerford manor by Bolingbroke; he is said to have worsted the French king in a duel near Calais in 1401 (which is not surprising: the king was Charles VI who was frequently off his head); he accompanied Henry V to France in 1415 with 80 men and fought bravely at Agincourt and was eventually created Baron Hungerford. His grandson Robert was taken prisoner at Castillon, a disaster for the English, at the end of the French wars in 1452 and remained a prisoner for seven years, whereupon on returning home he was just in time, as a Lancastrian, to be on the losing side and was attainted by Edward IV's first parliament: he was taken prisoner at Hexham and executed in 1464. His son Sir Thomas, although changing sides, was no luckier, because when he reverted to Henry VI's cause and supported Warwick's attempt to restore him, he was caught and executed at Salisbury, in 1469. His brother Robert, equally inconsistent, finally backed the right horse: he obtained a precarious pardon from Richard III which was withdrawn when Henry Tudor landed, but he escaped from custody, joined Henry, and at Bosworth killed Sir Robert Brackenbury, under whom he had previously served; he was knighted by the usurper on the battlefield and like Sir William Norris was rewarded by the restoration of his family's estates.

His son Sir Edward was a most unsavoury character. His second wife had murdered her husband in order to marry him, and ended up at Tyburn after his death; his son (by his first wife) was even worse. He was ambitious, procured from Thomas Cromwell several favours including a barony, treated his third wife with oustanding cruelty, and finally, entangled in an assortment of charges, was beheaded along with Cromwell in 1540. Their son Sir Walter had an appalling record of matrimonial troubles, finishing by marrying his mistress while his second wife, who he said had committed adultery and tried to poison him, was still alive.

Several related Hungerfords of the seventeenth century, all confusingly called Anthony, fought on both the Civil War sides. The son of one of them, Sir Edward, the last in the series, was knighted at Charles II's coronation. In 1669 his London house, Hungerford House, was burned down, whereupon he established a market on the site. The market house was removed in 1860 when Charing Cross Station was built: the bridge which carries the trains to the South Bank is still called Hungerford Bridge.

Hocktide used to be the occasion on which tithes were collected, in Hungerford, by officials called Tutti-men, who were also guardians of law and order before there was a police force. There is still a festival in the town each year based on the old custom.

The road up to the common passes the hospital, a large and functional but not entirely graceless building of 1840 which used to be the workhouse. The common is a wide open space on the hill-top overlooking the town: across it the lane takes the traveller through such tranquil, unhurried, undulating country as may be found all over the county. Inkpen, a village scattered around a network of lanes, is sequestered by enfolding trees and from the road up to the Downs is almost obscured by them.

These Downs are those of North Hampshire, a small pocket of which, by some peculiar boundary arrangement, is in Berkshire. A similar salient, further east, gives Calleva Atrebatum, which certainly ought to belong to Berkshire, to Hampshire, so perhaps one compensates for the other. Walbury Hill, the highest point of the Berkshire share, rises to 980 feet, so the climb up from Inkpen is a stiff one. On Inkpen Hill, directly above the village, there is a long barrow, and in the middle of it there is a tall pole with a cross-tree at the top. The barrow is the tomb of some Neolithic chieftain; the pole, Combe Gibbet, with the cross-bar able to cater for two, is more recent but has not been used for some considerable time.

The view from this height, on a clear day, is extraordinary: from the Wiltshire hills in the west right across the southern front of the Berkshire Downs to the Thames valley in the east, and looking southward, to the Portway and South Downs. To contemplate this vast panorama is to see the gentle, civilised landscape of old southern England and think about the 2,000 years or more that have gone by in its making; every century, almost every decade, has left something: a field pattern, a building, the positioning of a village, a highway. Close at hand on the higher hill to the east of the grim gibbet is an ineradicable relic of the beginning of those years: the huge, 82-acre hill-fort of Walbury, the biggest Iron Age defence work in Berkshire. When the men who made it stood and looked out over this landscape, they saw a savage, uncultured, new land; they knew that in the thick forests below them there were fierce wild animals, and that any strangers who ventured into their territory were to be feared, for they might be hostile. Countless generations have come and gone since then, millions of men and women who have each contributed in some tiny part to the making of the landscape, from the humblest digger of the ditches of Walbury to the little boy even now dropping his sweet-paper on it as he runs to catch up with his school party.

There is not much of Berkshire south of these heights, only two or three square miles, but they contain Combe, surely the loneliest village in the county, tucked away in the hills, sheltered by the great ridge, surrounded by protective trees. It comprises no more than a few farmsteads and cottages, and the usual church and manor-house, but even here the church shows that it was begun in that burst of building in stone in the late twelfth century, when Angevin government, strict, severe and hotly resented though it might have been, had brought peace, justice and prosperity to the land.

The road along the filled-in northern ditch of Walbury descends the hill and permits a swift gallop down to the outposts of Inkpen again, past Kirby House in a fold of the ground at the foot of the hill, a big rambling Georgian country-house, with lawns, elms and topiary before the graceful frontage of 1733, and a big extension behind 30 years later.

One of the many quarters of Inkpen is a sandy heathland, which must now be crossed on the way down to the river-levels of the Kennet and Kintbury (Kennet-bury) on its banks. It is not a greatly distinguished village but as usual its church shows the marks of successive generations, from the Norman south doorway to the Victorian nave roof, now tastefully painted in white, red and black, in a style reminiscent of Paddington Station. The Raymond family of Barton Court, just across the river, have left their mark with huge marble tombs with busts, coats of arms and panegyrics to departed members of the seventeenth and eighteenth centuries.

East from here up Irish Hill across the lonely corn-fields above the river, a lane approaches the park walls of Hamstead Marshall, the Earl of Craven's principal seat. It was shown in an earlier chapter how Craven, a wealthy man, had served and helped financially the Electress Elizabeth, Charles II's aunt, when the King would do nothing for her himself. Craven gave her his London house to live in, but eventually set about the rebuilding of his manor-house at Hamstead Marshall (so called because it had once been a manor of the Earl Marshal of England). He engaged the architect Sir Balthasar Gerbier, a native of Antwerp who had been knighted by Charles I, to design the new house so that Elizabeth could stay or visit there if she wished. Unfortunately Elizabeth died before it was finished, and Gerbier himself died shortly afterwards, in 1667. Ironically, considering Craven's fascination with fire-fighting, the house burned down in 1718, after his death. The only examples of Gerbier's work to survive are several sets of gate-piers, with flamboyant floral designs and either urns or pineapples on top, which can be passed through by using a footpath crossing the park. The little church, originally Norman but with much Decorated rebuilding and an eighteenth-century brick tower, was well restored in 1929: Gerbier is buried in it, with two sets of his gate-piers close at hand. Just east of the church are some overgrown 'castle mounds' which are probably the motte-and-bailey of the original manor-house; the fishponds created in the park by a dammed stream are also part of the mediaeval manor, and so is a tall conical mound on the far side of the lower one: a defence work of some kind, but of what date is not known. As part of the Earl Marshal's estate (William the Marshal, Earl of Pembroke, warrior for Henry II and Richard I, loyal supporter of John, regent for the young Henry III, one of the most highly respected men of his time) there would most likely be a castle with a garrison and accommodation for any army of levies, the collection of which in emergency was part of the earl's duties: there is no evidence of stone-work so they would have been wooden walls.

Where the fishpond stream falls into the Kennet a later lord of this manor built, in the early nineteenth century, a mill, now cream-painted, which has a central octagonal tower. It is probably contemporary with the present house, also cream-painted, a large slate-roofed mansion which displays the Craven arms but is now a nursing home.

A drive from Hamstead Marshall emerges opposite Enborne church, which has evidence of great age, possibly even pre-Conquest, and repairs and additions of most subsequent times including a fourteenth-century wall-painting. As I mentioned in connection with Chaddleworth, Dugdale quotes a ridiculous and salacious custom of these manors, which he takes from Tomlin's edition of Jacob's Law Dictionary (I regret that I have not personally seen this work).

> 'In the manors of East and West Enborne in the county of Berkshire . . . there is a custom, that when a copyhold tenant dies, his widow shall have her Free Bench in all his customary lands, *'dum sola et casta fuerit'* (as long as she shall continue sole and chaste); but if she commits incontinency, she forfeits her estate; yet nevertheless, on her coming into the court of the manor, riding backwards on a black ram, with his tail in her hand, and saying the words following, the Steward is bound by the custom to re-admit her to her Free-Bench:

Here I am, riding on a black Ram,
Like a Whore as I am;
And for my crincum crancum, I have lost my bincum bancum;
And for my Tail's Game, have done this worldly shame,
Therefore pray Mr Steward, let me have my land again.

The number of merry widows who availed themselves of this practice does not appear to be recorded.

The land from Enborne towards Wash Common and Newbury contains the gentle valley of another stream, a couple of farmsteads, much woodland, and the track of yet another stricken branch railway-line. On 20 September 1643 it was the scene of a bloody and hard-fought battle between the Royalists, under King Charles I himself, and a Parliamentary army commanded by the Earl of Essex (Robert Devereux, son of Elizabeth's ungrateful favourite).

The King's men had captured Bristol and Exeter, and only Gloucester remained in Parliamentary hands between the Bristol Channel and Manchester. Essex marched to relieve Gloucester, did so, and now had to return to London, through Royalist territory. He outmanoeuvred Charles, and although Prince Rupert and his cavalry were able to attack him on Aldbourne Chase, forcing him to move to the far side of the Kennet, the opportunity to destroy his army had been missed. The King nevertheless moved quickly to place his troops between Essex and London, and moved out of Newbury on the evening of the 19th to meet the Roundheads the next day. Charles had all the advantages.

Essex left his wagons in Hamstead Park and moved into position early in the morning of the 20th. The Royalists had failed to occupy a small hill, which Essex saw could be a tactical strongpoint, so he stationed some guns on it. When dawn came the Royalists found that their position was overlooked by the enemy, and the hardest fighting of the day consisted in the attempts to take the hill. A high hedge screened the Roundheads' infantry from the Royalists' view, with only a gap in it, and instead of trying to destroy the hedge they rode through the gap and suffered heavy casualties as a result. The first of them was Lucius Cary, Viscount Falkland, the King's secretary, a gentle, academic, rather pusillanimous man who was so depressed by a war whose coming he had expected that, incapable of imagining a way of ending it, he could only look for his own end. Riding through the gap in the hedge was tantamount to suicide, but nevertheless Falkland has been given a monument at the crossroads at Wash Common.

The fighting, involving the heaviest artillery duel of the war, swayed to and fro giving advantage first to one side, then to the other, but it was decided at last by the superior stubbornness of the Parliamentary infantry, the trained bands of London. Both sides withdrew, to count the cost. The King's army still stood between Essex and London, but he had come nowhere near destroying the Parliamentary troops. The King, moreover, was down to his last powder barrel, could do no more to harass Essex, and decided therefore to withdraw to Oxford. Essex moved on, keeping south of the Kennet, and although Rupert and his cavalry attacked him between Aldermaston and Padworth he beat them off, and on 28 September he and his men were in London. At no other time did Charles come closer to demolishing Parliamentary opposition: if the expected supply of powder had arrived in time from Oxford, and the fighting had continued into the next day, he might have routed Essex and been in a position to dictate terms to the Parliamentary leaders in London.

Before turning to Newbury, the country on the northern bank of the Kennet, around its confluence with the Lambourn, ought to be explored, beginning with Welford, on the Lambourn just north of the M4 motorway. Apart from a few cottages, including a row of former Berkshire style which have been cleverly rebuilt with tiles instead of thatch, there is little else to Welford but the church and manor-house, grouped together as usual but both comparatively recent. The manor-house, which has imposing wrought-iron gates, surmounted by a monogram and an armoured leg, is a big house of the late seventeenth century, refaced in the fashionable style of 50 years or so later. The church is entirely Victorian, of 1855, a replica, with round tower and spire, of the Norman church it may have replaced.

Under the M4 and up the other side, there is a view from near Boxford of Borough Hill, a small and much damaged hill-fort all covered by trees. A turning from the Lambourn road by the Bell inn under a bridge of the old railway which here at least still has rails, runs into Boxford, one of the prettiest villages in this region of the county. There is a former mill which, ivy-clad, protects a fine garden around the mill-race and the Georgian mill-house, a group of good timbered and thatched cottages, and a church which, although mainly Victorian, with an earlier brick tower, at least does not look out of place. A steep hill north-east of the village to Boxford Common emerges from the trees to a sheltered shallow valley where in a corn-field on the left of the road a Roman farmstead once existed.

Winterbourne manor-house and church stand on another tree-covered hill-top, and while not outstanding themselves (the church mainly Victorian, the manor-house late Georgian, in brick, although the rear part is timbered and could be much earlier) provide another example, first, of the typical headsman's axe type of ancient siting, and secondly of a migrated village, because all the cottages of Winterbourne are at the bottom of the hill along the course of the eponymous stream. True to its title, in this driest of dry summers, there is nothing drier than the stream-bed. Water being essential to life, it is likely that the cottagers, if they ever did live on the hill-top near the church, moved down to the valley nearer to it. It might be interesting to know if the manor ever had a name preceding Winterbourne.

On the other side of the Bourne valley is Snelsmore Common, a heavily forested ridge in which there is an ancient earthwork of uncertain date called Black Ditch. On the other side of the A34, replete as usual with traffic frenetically heading for Newbury or Oxford, is more thick greenwood and among the trees, the scattered houses of Curridge, which seems to be growing into a garden-city kind of place. Much of this country, in fact, supports the working population of Newbury and is a kind of miniature commuter-belt: the same can be said of Hermitage, which exists over a wide area, through the middle of which the Newbury to Didcot railway-line runs like some recently-dead ghost, not old enough to be reckoned a part of historical antiquity.

The eastern hillside and ridge of the railway valley at Hermitage is covered by a wide expanse of woodland, in the middle and at the highest peak of which is an Iron Age fort called Grimsbury (who else's? It was there when we, the Saxons, came, so no human could have made it!). The walls and ditches are not in as good condition as, say, Membury, but are still discernible beneath their mantle of tall trees. The road runs right across the middle of the fort, and within the ramparts near the road is a little Victorian brick tower, with a conical roof, inhabited as a house.

The commuter-belt extends through Cold Ash to Ashmore Green, where a long and winding lane descends from the car-and-garden country to the valley of the Kennet, the town of Newbury, and Shaw, its northern suburb. Shaw House, which is now a girls' school, is a mighty and magnificent Elizabethan mansion, the biggest in Berkshire, and the fact that it was built for a clothier, Thomas Dolman, tells all that needs to be known of the wealth which could accrue to an enterprising entrepreneur in the making of woollen cloth in late Tudor England.

The Lambourn, nearing its confluence with the Kennet, flows down to Shaw from Donnington, nowadays also more or less a suburb of Newbury. Until the fairly recent construction of a new route for the A34 Oxford road, to cross the Lambourn near Shaw church, it approached Newbury through Donnington, and for that reason a castle was built on the edge of the ridge of hills west of the road. The grant of a licence to crenellate to Sir Robert de Abbesbury in 1386 was part of an attempt to strengthen the southern defences of England against a possible French invasion: the castle at Bodiam, Sussex, was built at the same time. Donnington had very much the same kind of design as Bodiam, a quadrangle with high walls, round corner towers, square intermediate towers and a huge gatehouse with its own round towers. Inside there were only timber buildings. The gatehouse is all that remains now, but probably more of the original walls stood in 1644, when it acted in the purpose for which it was intended, to guard the road to Oxford: except that, instead of Frenchmen trying to break through, the attackers were Englishmen.

Since the first battle of Newbury, the fortunes of the struggle between the King and his Parliament had fluctuated: the Royalists had relieved the garrison of Newark, deprived Waller of all his guns at Cropredy Bridge and Essex of most of his army at Lostwithiel, but had been soundly beaten at Cheriton and at Marston Moor, as a result of which last action the north was lost to the King.

On his way back from the success in Cornwall against Essex, the King found that his way to Oxford was blocked by a large Roundhead force near Newbury, just as he himself had barred the way to Essex over a year before. The King, in possession of Newbury, took up a position north of the town, covering the strong-points at Speen, Donnington and Shaw House. The Earl of Manchester, commanding the Parliamentary army, detached Waller with 12,000 men to make a flanking attack on the Royalist left at Speen, while he engaged them at Shaw House. Waller's men fought hard against the Royalists under Prince Rupert's brother, Maurice, and captured Speen, but failed to break through the line; Manchester failed also to take Shaw House (some of the earthen embankments that the Royalists threw up can still be seen there), and the Royalists remained undefeated. The King, however, did not consider his position good enough to hold any longer, since his forces were greatly inferior in numbers, and early the next day, 28 October, he made his way up the road to Oxford. Such modest success as the second battle of Newbury offered was the King's last in command: the following June was the time of Naseby and total disaster.

Speen, the scene of the hardest fighting, is now an undistinguished suburb of Newbury: some good eighteenth-century houses still stand, however, one of which, Benham Park, was built and the gardens laid out by the redoubtable Capability Brown for the 6th Earl of Craven. But Speen has one of the oldest names in the county: it is a rare case of the Saxons adopting an existing name, for their *Spene* (821) is derived from the Romans' settlement of *Spinae,* which in turn is their version of the Britons' *Spian,* which means in the Celtic tongue, 'place of thorn-bushes'.

According to Leland, Newbury, with Abingdon and Reading, was one of the three most important cloth towns of Berkshire. Ample evidence of the money to be made out of it is provided for Elizabethan times by the extravagant mansion, fit for an aristocrat, which Thomas Dolman was able to build at Shaw. His most celebrated predecessor was John Smallwood, alias John of Winchcombe (in Gloucestershire), alias Jack of Newbury; he had married a widow whose cloth manufactory he had managed, and when he had full control extended it to run, it was said, 100 looms. His success became proverbial, his fame widespread. He made enough money to build, not a fine house, but the best part of a new parish church. St Nicholas, Newbury, is a splendid church, in the high, light and airy climactic excellence of mediaeval architecture. Jack of Newbury paid for the nave: he and his wife are commemorated by a brass in the tower room, which says:

'Of your Charity pray for the Soule of John Smalwode, alias Winchcom, and Alice his wife, Which John died the 15th day of February, An.Dom. 1519.'

The church was not finished until about 1532; the two Gothic archways from the street to the churchyard are not contemporaneous; they were added in about 1770.

A house in Northbrook Street, over the pretty, one-arched bridge and along on the right, is said to have been the Smallwoods'; it is now a shop, Nos 23-24, and the front over the shop façade has been plastered and painted, but there is a side-alley from which the end of the gable can be seen, timber-framed, brick-nogged, with a jetty (overhang) and an oriel window. If the Horseshoe Cloisters in Windsor Castle, erected at some date after 1475, are borne in mind, then this could quite easily be a late fifteenth-century house and therefore could have belonged to the champion clothier.

The church is without doubt the finest monument to the town's affluence at the height of the cloth-trade, but plenty of fine buildings which followed in its wake have also survived and help to give Newbury its present character. In Wharf Street, off the north of the Market Place, there is the Cloth Hall, built in 1626 to give employment to the poor as a sort of municipal workshop: it is now the Town Museum. A visit to it costs nothing and is warmly recommended, because it is a very good museum. Its exhibits are not limited to Newbury but show evidence of the history of Berkshire from the Old Stone Age through all the changing scenes of life, and including finds from the Mesolithic settlement at nearby Thatcham, Roman, Saxon and mediaeval relics, agricultural implements of the nineteenth century, and a whole section showing the natural history of the region.

One exhibit, complete with pictures, placards and the whole story, is the Throckmorton Coat, which used to be kept in the Throckmortons' family seat, Buckland House. This ordinary-looking blue tail-coat in woollen cloth was the result of an exchange of opinions between Sir John Throckmorton and one George Coxeter, clothier of Newbury, concerning the probabilities of producing a finished article from start to finish in one day. The challenge having been made, very early one morning in the year 1811, certain of Sir John's sheep were shorn, and during the day all the successive necessary processes – spinning the wool into yarn, weaving it into cloth, cleaning it, fulling, dyeing, cutting and tailoring it into a garment – were accomplished so that, in a time of 13 hours, 20 minutes precisely from start to finish, Sir John was able to put the coat on and wear it at dinner.

Yet Dugdale, only a few years later, was writing that 'the clothing trade . . . has long left the town, for the more western parts of the kingdom, and at present nothing but serge is manufactured here . . .'. Fortunately, like Hungerford, there was the canal, which had already been dug from Newbury to Reading and whose extension all the way to Bristol was completed in 1810, and this brought the corn trade into prominence, for grain was just the kind of commodity to be carried most economically by water. The Corn Store, behind the Museum in Wharf Street, is a long timber-framed building intended originally, most likely, for wool, since it was built in the late seventeenth century, but near enough to the new canal conveniently to be adapted. The Corn Exchange, in the Market Place, was built in 1862, substantially in stone, which shows that business was booming then (as it was in most parts of the country in those years). There was also the town's situation in close proximity to the Bath road, running north of the river through Speen, so Newbury did not suffer such great privations as might otherwise have been the case from the decline in the cloth-trade. Now there are dozens of different industries in addition to agriculture, not to mention the race-course.

Through one of the peripheral industrial estates a way can be found to the canal, and the footpath, formerly the towpath, along its side. Above the bridge there are boats, but this section below Newbury is at present choked with weeds and clearly unnavigable, the locks unworkable. But, that being the case, both canal and towpath are invaluable as a peaceful retreat from all the noisy activity around them, from the railway and factories on one side and the noisy Bath road on the other; here is vivid greenness in the arid summer, all kinds of water-life, fish, waterfowl, dragonflies, butterflies, and for the angler sitting on the bank or the walker along the path, here is cool serenity, 'a green thought in a green shade'.

Beyond where the railway crosses the canal there are one or two concrete machine-gun posts, on the north side of the canal: there are many of these structures still dotted around southern England, since they are practically indestructible. What is made by man and cannot easily be unmade is usually left alone, whether it is a massive hill-fort or a small but thick concrete box.

Either the towpath can be followed all the way to Thatcham station, or a footpath taken across the marshes, the railway and the gravel-works to a road into the village. On the last stage of the latter way, the path to the road, it might as well be remembered that once, not much more than 8,000 years ago, there existed in the vicinity a settlement of people. The river-level gave rise to a small lake, and Mesolithic hunters had cleared the trees on its shores to make a simple living-space. No trace of hutments have been found, so presumably they were unable to rise to that form of comfort, but their hearths, some tools, and other oddments were found by excavation, and from the evidence it was reckoned that the site was used intermittently for about 1,000 years.

The village of Thatcham has been occupied for a similar period (its name, recorded in 970, means 'a thatched homestead') and has recently been augmented by a considerable quantity of new building. It has a large and mainly Victorian church on a piece of rising ground, and a wide High Street with a central green, where no doubt the two annual fairs were held in times past. On the Bath road, at a corner where the road goes off northwards to the hills, is a small building which has stone and flint lower walls, stone quoins, and early seventeenth-century windows with dripstones. It was founded as a chapel, apparently in 1304, and was in a state of decay when bought by Lady Frances Winchcomb in 1707 as a charity school which still functioned in Dugdale's time.

The hills to which the road from Thatcham heads, are another region of Newbury's commuter-belt, judging by the houses around the roads of Upper Bucklebury. The common on its northern side is typical heathland which gives way as the land slopes down to the valley of the Pang to good arable farmland, heralded by Winchcombe Farm. Bucklebury proper is a tiny, sleepy village on the Pang, no more than a cluster of cottages, some of which are in the timber-framed, brick-nogged, thatched style which is normal in Berkshire, a large brick rectory of the early eighteenth century and the church. It is a flint church, with a very good decorated Norman south doorway to show when it was first built, and additions in later times such as the thirteenth-century arcade, the Perpendicular tower, and the lovely soft-glowing coloured windows in the chancel, by the artist Brangwyn in 1912. There is a beam above the communion rail on which is written: '1591 + Francis Winchecom Esquier build this'; below the beam on one side are crested helms, gauntlets and swords, and on the other side a memorial tablet to a Sir Henry Winchcombe of the seventeenth century. Dugdale says that the Winchcombes were granted the manor, which had previously belonged to Reading Abbey, in 1539, and that the recipient, John Winchcombe, was the son of the famous Jack of Newbury. His name was Smallwood, so unless Dugdale is wrong he appears to have found the name Winchcombe more suited to a person of his wealth and station.

From Bucklebury the lane meanders through some very pleasant hilly country on the edges of the Pang valley, which is shallow, peaceful, and supports little more than woods, meadows, and arable fields. The lane arrives, along with the stream, at Stanford Dingley, another attractive village with a green, shady oaks on it, weathered old cottages around it (but unless it harbours a more convincingly mediaeval interior, I do not believe the Bull inn's claim to be fifteenth-century: although bricks were used in Berkshire far earlier than in most counties, even for such humble buildings as this, the style, not timbered, looks much later). It has an old and pretty church on a rise north of the village, unusually dedicated to the French St Denys, built mainly of flint with a weatherboarded bell-turret, arcades of the twelfth century (north) and thirteenth (south) and the remains, high up on the walls, of thirteenth-century mural paintings.

The chancel was added, in brick, in 1768.

On the north side of the river now, the lane runs peacefully to Bradfield. Across the quiet valley and the small Pang, a cluster of russet roofs lead the eye up to the dominant buildings of Bradfield School. The Victorian Gothic architecture in flint and red brick has settled down, weathered, and become part of the scenery, in tune with the cottages of the village, several of which are good Georgian houses. Most of them seem to have something to do with the school, which often happens: a school needs an army of staff to cope with cooking, cleaning, gardening and all the other administrative jobs, and a whole village can be drawn into it.

Bradfield School was founded by the Reverend Thomas Stevens, squire and rector of the village, in 1850. He was one of those who pursue an aim without seriously considering whether or not it is possible to finance it. Stevens used the site of his own manor-house (small fragments of which remain) and began to build his school around it. Within 30 years he was ruined, his manor and lands sold, his rectory sequestrated; but the school survived, gained in stature, and began to flourish. More buildings, including a Greek theatre, were added in the 1890s, and more houses acquired.

A ridge of hills lies between Bradfield and the Kennet, and on the lower slopes of it are the park and lands of Englefield House. It is a useful reflection on the state of extreme confusion in post-Roman Britain that among the Saxons who settled in south-east England, mingling with the resident Celts here and there (as, perhaps, at East Shefford: if the cemetery really is early Christian then it is possible that the Saxon settlers were converted by the Britons; there is no proof) and occasional detached tribes of Angles. Englefield is derived from '*Engla feld*', as recorded in 871, when the Anglo-Saxon Chronicle tells of ealdorman Aethelwulf's victory there against a body of Danes, and means 'field of the Angles': there is another Englefield on the borders of Surrey, south of Old Windsor, and if Dugdale is right Hungerford's old name may have the same meaning. 'Angliae' is in fact the Latin version of the generic name for these Germanic people: in view of the present name, England, and these occasional place-names, it is probably correct to speak of them as Engles rather than Angles.

Englefield village was moved away to a new site by emparkment: not far, but far enough to put a little distance between church and cottages. The big house was probably built late in Elizabeth's reign after it had been confiscated from Sir Francis Englefield, who was a Catholic. It was remodelled when Sir George Gilbert Scott rebuilt the church, and again when in 1886 there was a fire. From a distance it looks, with all the towers, pinnacles and minarets, thoroughly Victorian.

On the far side of the Kennet by Newbury, the county boundary closes in: it is represented by the little River Enborne, which rises in the North Hampshire Downs below Warbury, with only a ridge between it and the Kennet. Between Greenham, on the edge of the ridge just outside Newbury, and Crookham, the two or three miles of land are occupied principally by the runways of R.A.F. Greenham, a fighter squadron. The noise is tremendous, but it is fascinating to watch the aircraft landing and taking off, and admire the professional skill of the pilots. The airfield stretches over what used to be Greenham Common, and much of the land on the ridge, typical of the geological formation of basically chalky country, is sandy heath-land. Crookham consists of a few scattered cottages and houses on the heath, and the ridge road, having wriggled round the perimeter of the airfield, now goes straight across the common to Brimpton. Near here the Enborne, relieved of its frontier responsibilities, turns north and makes for the Kennet, and the land declines to the river-levels. The church is a Victorian reconstruction, in flint (even used to face the brick tower of 1748), but at Manor Farm, a short way down the lane towards the Kennet, there is a small mediaeval chapel, also in flint, of Norman origin, with additions of later centuries. As we have seen, there were times when two manors in one original settlement developed their own churches and sometimes, as in the case of the Astons, split into two parishes. At Brimpton the second church remained a mere chapel to the manor-house and the first became the parish church.

Across the Enborne on its way to Aldermaston the lane passes by the grounds of Wasing Place, a good-looking house rebuilt in the same style and from the materials of the previous occupant of the site, burnt out during the 1939-1945 war. Nearby, running across the north of the park the agger of a Roman road has been found; on the Kennet at Brimpton there was recorded in the 10th century a 'weala brucge', or wala-bridge; possibly this name represented the remains of a Roman bridge, and if so it would be on the spot where Ermin Street would have crossed the Kennet, heading through Wasing Park on its way to Calleva.

The village of Aldermaston stretches from its inn, at one end, up the street to the lodge gates of the former manor-house at the other. Its church, nearly half a mile up another lane, is still near the manor-house: an example, in all probability, again of the removal of a village by emparkment. Dugdale records that the house was rebuilt in 1636 (the lodges are certainly of around this date) by Sir Humphrey Foster: it was a time when wealthy landowners were rebuilding and improving their social status by creating for themselves great country mansions and parks instead of the manor-houses and arable land which they had either inherited or, as in many cases, bought. It was the time following the mercantile expansion of Elizabeth's reign, when the merchants became 'gentry' and, as tax-paying Members of Parliament, felt confident enough to challenge the King's government. The cottages of Aldermaston ('the tun of the ealdorman') are in brick, of the seventeenth and eighteenth centuries. The inn has a gable, a clock and a bell-turret, the village now has a working potter, and the park of Aldermaston Court (which was burnt down in 1843 and rebuilt in Victorian Tudor) supports an establishment of the Atomic Energy Authority, which used to attract the attention of the Campaign for Nuclear Disarmament.

From the hilly lane on the way from Aldermaston to Padworth there is a good view of the valley of the Kennet, a delightful sight with the tree-lined ridge on the other side and the river and canal set about with many poplars and ashes. Flirting with the county boundary again, a path crosses the heathy birch, bracken and gorse-covered country to Padworth Common. On the top of this ridge, facing north, there can be seen remains of some defensive earthworks, known as Grim's Bank. The site of Calleva Atrebatum, the cantonal capital of the region of Roman Britain occupied by the Atrebates, is not far to the south, and roads radiate from it in all directions. The earthworks appear to defend two of them: that called Ermin Street, and another running almost due north in the direction of Dorchester-on-Thames. It is thought that they were erected at a time when early Saxon infiltration of the Thames valley had slowed down, perhaps after the British victory at *Mons Badonicus* (wherever that might have been) and a British enclave still survived at Calleva: the ditches would serve the two-fold purpose of marking the boundary between Saxon-held territory and that remaining to the Britons, and perhaps also providing defensive cover against Saxon attack, should it occur. After the next phase of Saxon expansion, in the middle of the 6th century, British occupation of Calleva seems to have come to an end.

This lane across the centre of the ridge, between Aldermaston and Padworth Common and running on to Burghfield Common, is probably the one on which Essex's tattered army was attacked by Prince Rupert's cavalry after the first battle of Newbury, in September 1643. Before leaving Newbury, Prince Rupert is supposed to have made the following pun, saying that 'although the Roundheads were marching unto Reading they would make calves of many of them before they came unto the Veale' (Theale). It was a near thing, but the Roundheads were saved by the fire-power and discipline of their infantry, who fired volleys from the hedges and drove off the Royalists.

Grim's Bank is rather mixed nowadays with some less archaeologically interesting earthworks connected with some pipe-line installations. On the far side of them is Padworth, a few cottages, a lovely little Norman church with an apsidal chancel and faint signs of a painting on the east wall of the nave, and Padworth House, north of the church, a Georgian house of 1769. Down by the river there is also what used to be a charming little fishing lodge, with a 'Gothick' façade and embattled gables, but it is derelict and moribund.

A track from Old Farm, Padworth, dives into thick woods for a glimpse of Ufton Court, a late sixteenth-century house with many gables, L-shaped, white-painted, standing high over a wood-encircled terraced garden with descending dammed pools. Francis Perkins, who built it, was a determined Catholic, so he devised no less than three ingeniously concealed compartments into which a priest might go should the Queen's officers come searching.

The old house is in the parish of Ufton Nervet, the village and church of which are about half a mile distant. The two elements of the name are, as usual, Saxon and Norman respectively, but the second part has undergone a slight alteration. 'Uffa's tun' was held in 1242 by Richer Neyrnut, a name described earlier in 1207 as Neirenuit and in 1236 in Latin as Nigranox, all of which are variations of 'Black night'; for some reason the second 'n' changed to 'v' to form Nervet. The parish church, in nineteenth-century Decorated style (quite good, with a shingled broach spire with dormers), shelters behind a yew tree which must have been growing when the church's predecessor existed, if not when it was erected.

Across the road from the church, Ufton Place is an interesting and to my mind successful modern attempt at the grace and elegance of Georgian domestic architecture; it is in yellow brick, with a pillared portico, a pediment with sculpted heraldic figures, sash windows placed symmetrically, and a tiny 'landscaped' garden complete with pond and bridge.

Sulhamstead is a widely scattered place with earlier manors bearing the names of their tenants as suffixes: Abbots, of the Abbot of Reading, and Bannister, held by William Banastre in 1198. Both of them have a church, that at Abbots originally late Norman, and at the part of the village called simply Sulhamstead, on the hill extending down to the Kennet level, there is a house developed twice by Lutyens for different owners, one wanting a William-and-Mary styled place attached to an old timbered cottage, the next (in 1912) preferring the Arts and Crafts country style. It is called Folly Farm.

At the bottom of the hill, on the lane leading to the huge white-painted mansion now used as a police training school, there is an excellent box-framed farmhouse called Brazenhead: it is H-shaped, two joined cross-wings, tiled and brick-infilled, and dates from the early seventeenth century.

The riverside water-meadows of the Kennet here are more water than meadow, because most of them have been excavated for gravel and have therefore become lakes. The longer established ones are now tree-lined and picturesque, and, in place of the grazing cattle and sheep of former days, support sundry aquatic diversions. There are no more calves before we come unto the Veale.

EIGHT

Loddon

This chapter concerns not only the part of the Loddon valley that lies between the Hampshire border and the M4 but also some of the country on either side of it, from Burghfield Common in the west to Bramshill Forest in the east. There is far more building, on the whole, all over this tract of country, but still the contrast persists, between urban urgency in one part and bucolic beatitude not half a mile away in another.

Burghfield Common is on the same heathy ridge as Padworth and Ufton Nervet, and bears out the statement in the first paragraph, because it consists of a tremendous area of housing on the edge of an extensive forest, mainly coniferous. Lanes across it through Brewery Common fail to reveal a brewery but arrive at the large green of Mortimer; rather uninteresting Victorian houses surround it and with more modern additions flank the road to its parent village Stratfield Mortimer.

Its name is one of the most interesting things about this otherwise somewhat unmemorable place: in it are represented memories of three separate ages. Stratfield is its Saxon name, recalling the 'Field on the Roman road', one of the radial roads out of Calleva which, although untraceable except in theory now, ran towards Reading along the valley of the little Foudry Brook. The Saxon settlement became in the eleventh century the manor of Radulf de Mortemer, the tenant recorded in Domesday Book.

The Foudry Brook is currently a meagre brown stream, and the parish church is a Victorian structure of 1869 and is furthermore kept locked, but inside it, according to Pevsner, is another reminder of Saxon days, a coffin-lid with an inscription referring to one Aegelward, who died in 1017 and is allegedly mentioned in the Anglo-Saxon Chronicle. The only person similar in name, recorded as having been slain in the year 1017, when Cnut became king of all England, is 'Aethelweard, son of Aethelmaer the Stout': if this Aegelward is the same person as Aethelweard, then the inscription is useful and valuable.

The railway, which still runs along the valley from Reading, is no doubt responsible for the late-Victorian development of the village: the easy journey made it possible for many people to move out of town, into the country, and still get to work in the town. The principle of commuting was born.

Up the hill and over it to Beech Hill the winding lanes bring the traveller to the ridge west of the lovely levels of Loddon, a river plain of gentle Arcadian beauty, green even in the drought; Beech Hill is a small community on the slight rise commanding this delectable view. It is only a mile north of the county boundary with Hampshire, which here and for some distance until it crosses the Blackwater river is provided by the Roman road from Calleva to London called by the Saxons the Devil's Highway.

Dense woodland crowds the lane down to the Loddon which is a small but pretty stream. A little way downstream the river is crossed by the A33, once the turnpike road from Reading to Basingstoke, which passes through Three Mile Cross, just south of the modern M4, and Swallowfield, near this crossing of the Loddon. Both of them were inhabited by an important literary figure of the nineteenth century, Mary Russell Mitford.

Mary was born in Alresford, Hampshire, in 1787, the only child of a selfish, indolent and extravagant man who spent most of his life living off his daughter. This was at first easy because at the age of 10 she won a lottery prize worth £20,000. Mary was a voracious reader and she was able to go to school in London and later, at home with her parents, she began to write and publish poetry. In 1820 all the money had gone and the family moved to a threadbare cottage in Three Mile Cross. Mary stayed there for 30 years, and it was here that she wrote, more and more, her parents depending on what she could

18 & 19 Reading: *above* The Abbey gateway; *below* St Mary's Church

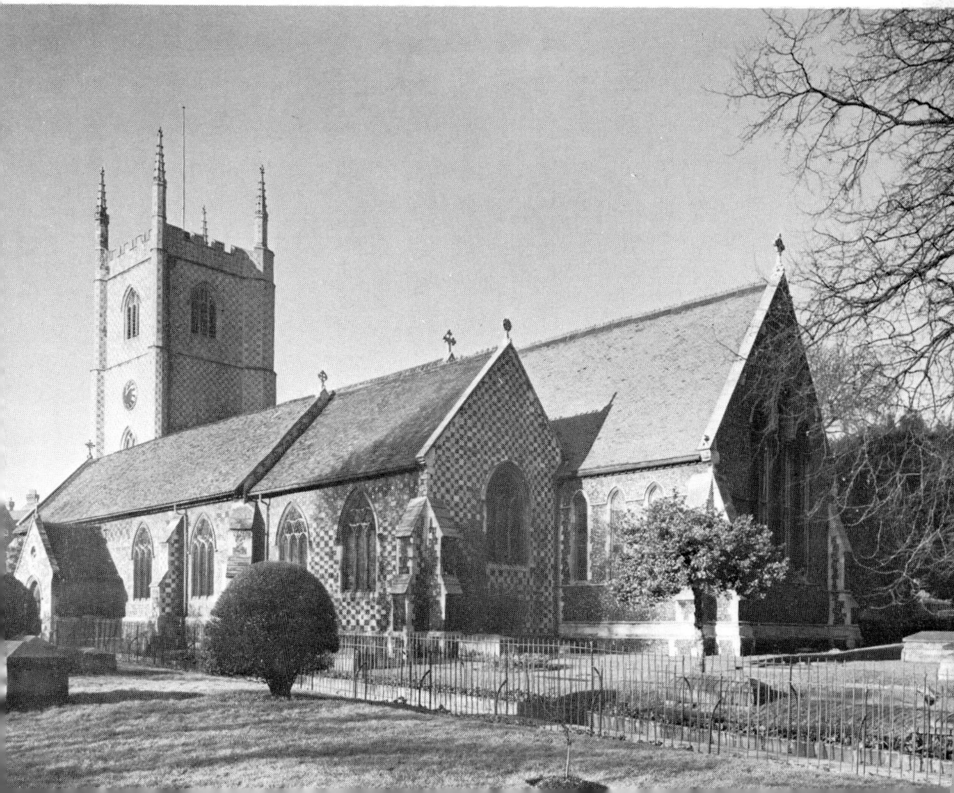

earn to keep them; at first she wrote for magazines, but Coleridge encouraged her (evidently mistakenly) to write dramatic tragedy. Several of her plays were produced and acted, but none made much impression and all were quickly forgotten. Then she began to write a series of sketches, the first of which had already appeared in 1819 in *The Lady's Magazine*, about the countryside around her. Called collectively *Our Village,* these sketches initiated a branch of literature hitherto neglected: a study of the countryside and its life in accurate detail, with humour and lucidity. As time went on the sketches became increasingly popular and brought her attention (she became friendly with Elizabeth Barrett) and rewards, most of which were spent by her father. In 1842 he at last died, and such was Mary's fame that his debts were met by public subscription. She moved to Swallowfield in 1851 and lived there for the last four years of her life.

Swallowfield today, beset as it is by the main road, has so much new building that Mary Russell Mitford would probably not recognise it, although away from the road her gentle, affectionate descriptions of the landscape are still apt. Swallowfield Park, which was rebuilt by the second Earl of Clarendon, son of Charles II's Lord Chancellor, is out of sight behind its park trees, and the parish church is in a corner of its grounds, bearing witness to the village's desertion of its precincts for the more profitable proximity to the turnpike road. The church stands on the banks of the Blackwater river, which joins the Loddon on the other side of the Park, and apparently paradoxically accounts for the name of the village. What connection could there possibly be between Swallowfield and Blackwater? nominally at present, none, but the fact is that the river used to be called the Swale, an Old English word meaning 'whirling, rushing river'; the bird, swallow, has the same derivation because it is a whirling, rushing bird, so the two join in a typically muddled English way in Swallowfield, the 'field on the Swale'. The church is of flint, a restored Norman and Decorated building, and Mary Russell Mitford is said to be buried in the churchyard: anyone with more time than I was able to devote may be able to find her gravestone among the many others.

A short, quiet lane approaches Farley Hill, and affords a good view of Farley Hall, a splendid, long, low range of buildings of about 1730,

20 & 21 Along the Thames: *above* Marlow Bridge; *below* Brunel's railway bridge at Maidenhead

with a white lantern cupola rising above a central porch, all against a background of dark trees, which cover the whole hill. A network of lanes connects the constituent parts of the village, all set about among the trees, including the early nineteenth-century Gothick Farley Castle, which is now a school. On the way down from the hill to the main road A327, Hall's Farmhouse is worth a study: it is a brick house of about 1675 in an early classical style but with a sparse appearance because the spaces between the windows are the same size as the windows themselves, looking as if they were blocked up. Pevsner calls this 'artisan mannerism'.

A huge area east of the A327 from here is covered by Arborfield Garrison, a depot and training camp of the R.E.M.E. It is typically well-organised, clean and tidy, every effort having apparently been made to cater for the needs of all ranks and their families. There are times when it seems that Her Majesty's Services are almost the only sources of sanity, order and efficiency, nowadays.

Arborfield Cross is a hill-top hamlet at a meeting of the turnpike road with three others: it is consequently well-established, with two inns, one a timber-framed house, and opposite another still older (it looks early sixteenth-century) called the Old Post House, a name which tells its own story. Keeping for the time being to the A327 down to the Loddon level, it is possible to reach the early site of Arborfield by a lane to a pleasant pond-side settlement, and a farm track to Arborfield Hall Farm, by the river. On the left of it are the remains of the old church, a few flint walls and the shell of a brick chapel on the north side, all ivy-grown and romantically atmospheric with its old yews and gravestones still surrounding it. The brick wall alongside the churchyard is the only survivor of 'the old house at Aberleigh' described by Mary Russell Mitford. It was the manor-house, as can be deduced by its site near the church, and the village of Arborfield had long since moved away from it, seduced like Swallowfield by the lure of the turnpike road's traffic. Some of the present village stands along the lane by the modern Victorian church (of 1863), and if the lane is followed to the B3030 road which goes to Winnersh, there is a chance of taking a delightfully cool, leafy walk through the woods of Bear Wood. A few glimpses through the trees reveal the lake and mighty mansion created by John Walter, owner of

The Times, between 1865 and 1870. The estate had been bought in 1830 by John Walter II: his son John Walter III joined with the architect Robert Kerr in constructing this 'epitome of High Victorian domestic planning' as Pevsner calls it: part Jacobean, part Gothic, part French château, it has a huge tower, pinnacles, gables, turrets, all in red brick with stone dressings. It is now the Royal Merchant Navy School.

In 1870 the lake froze over, and on Christmas Eve the two sons of John Walter III and their cousin went skating on it. The ice broke, and the elder boy, who would have been John Walter IV, drowned trying to rescue the other two. The church on the other side of the lane nearest the mansion, built in 1846, has a monument to him. The Walter Arms inn and most of the houses at Sindlesham, which today lurks uncomfortably close to the M4, were built in the same Jacobean style by Walter, who on his estate established workshops for producing the woodwork, bricks, stone and even gas for all this construction.

James Vincent thought that the name Bear Wood derived from bears at large in it, but there is no record of such animals being found at the time when the Saxons settled and bestowed the majority of the place-names in the county: I would suggest that it is more probably from *baēr*, which is a woodland pig-pasture.

South of Bear Wood, Barkham extends along a street with several timber-framed cottages and at the end, a big white Georgian house called Barkham Square. In order to avoid the mass of housing in the vicinity of Wick Hill, it is possible to take the lane back in the direction of Arborfield Garrison, which skirts the wood Long Moor and joins the beginning of the long straight road called Ninemile Ride; it quickly leaves it and there is a southward lane that winds and climbs through farmland to the crossroads which the village of Finchampstead used to occupy before it began to cluster around the road from Wokingham to Basingstoke. There remains an inn and some cottages, and high on a bank above the road, the church: from the gate there is a wonderful view of the rolling, thickly afforested country to the south. The church was built in the late twelfth century, and its apse and tub-shaped font survive, but the windows were replaced at various architectural stages in later years and the tower was either added or replaced in 1720 with bricks laid in 'English bond' (alternate courses of headers and stretchers). The church has a coat of arms of Charles II, and the banner, which hung over his stall in the Henry VII Chapel in Westminster Abbey until 1919 when he died, of General Sir John Watson, V.C., G.C.B. He was a member of the family who lived in East Court, nearby, but only spent the last years of his life there because he had spent 38 years of it in India. It is fashionable these days to despise and execrate those who assisted an imperialist government to exploit the downtrodden slaves of some pillaged and ravished colony, but it is a reasonable bet that men like Sir John would not have thought that they were doing anything of the sort: they had old-fashioned ideas of duty and service, both to their country and to the people they were sent to govern. Many of them followed the example set them by Warren Hastings, who resisted every temptation to exploit the colony for his own ends, insisting on inflexible incorruptibility on his own and his staff's account.

The road to Basingstoke crosses the Blackwater river, which here is the county boundary; a lane a short distance from it follows a parallel course on the lowest rim of the valley hillside, giving views of the tree-lined river and the Hampshire hills on its far side. Near Sandhurst there are lakes produced by gravel extraction. The first building of Sandhurst to be seen from this approach is its church, which was completely rebuilt by Street in 1853 in sandstone, in an Early English style. The remains of Sandhurst before it became a town (subsequent to the arrival of the railway) are close at hand, but give way quickly to the expansion of the last hundred years or so. On the far side, before the road reaches the Royal Military Academy, which distinguishes the extreme south-eastern corner of Berkshire, there is a lane which climbs quietly in a straight line through Owlsmoor, a ribbon of houses with, now, a modern school, to a stretch of moorland and then to the forest.

The lane continues to Crowthorne but there is a barrier, a fence, and a footpath which edges away eastward, to the woods: across the skyline like a red-brick fortress stands Broadmoor Hospital.

The footpath enters the forest, beyond the confines of the hospital, by a lovely little woodland pond, created by a dammed stream, with another higher up: then the forest, Bramshill Forest, begins. The trees, for the most part, are dark battalions of pines, rank upon rank, column upon column, in gloomy succession; soon the path crosses the so-called Devil's Highway, and there is no mistaking that authoritative drive through all obstacles, over hill and dale, a road of 1,900 years' seniority, or more.

At a height of over 400 feet which, before the forest grew to such a coniferous mass must have been a commanding position, the path crosses the defensive rampart of 'Caesar's Camp', which as usual is nothing to do with Julius Caesar but is another Iron Age plateau fort in which, admittedly, among debris from that early period there has been found some Roman pottery. The rampart and ditch can be plainly seen all round, but best at the northern end where they are covered in tall and clean-limbed beeches.

If anyone wishes to approach Bracknell from Caesar's Camp, let him beware, for the map is set to nought by a succession of vastly disruptive housing estates, which have obliterated roads and practically everything else. There are huge quantities of houses in Bracknell New Town, but there do not appear to be too many shops, pubs, libraries, halls, sports grounds, or any other normal oppidan attributes. Bracknell itself is also still in the throes of alterations, and cannot be described with justice.

NINE

Thames-Side

The attractions of a spit of land between the confluence of two rivers for a settlement are clear: water is available for sustenance and for defence, and the remaining neck of land is fairly easily fortified. These advantages have evidently occurred to people from the very earliest times, since flint tools have been found on the site of one, Reading, belonging to types identified by the terms Chellean, Acheulian and Mousterian (which means that the flints correspond with examples found at Chelles, St Acheul and Le Moustier, in France). This provides a date of 400,000 B.C. at the latest for human habitation of the site.

There are subsequent relics of the New Stone Age, the Bronze Age and the Iron Age, and substantial evidence that in Roman times there was a considerable settlement on the site: two coin hoards of the late 4th century, a cemetery of similar date and pottery over a long period point to the possible use of the site as a river-port for Calleva Atrebatum; as appeared in the last chapter, there is no tangible evidence of a road from the cantonal capital to Reading, but there is the name Stratfield directly on its probably track. There are traces of Saxon cemeteries using both cremation (pre-Christian) and inhumation, so early occupation by the incoming settlers seems likely, especially on so conspicuous a site in the Thames valley, the most obvious invasion route. The existing Romano-British buildings may not have been used by the Saxons: John Wacher, in his *The Towns of Roman Britain,* argues reasonably that the Saxons tended not to occupy existing towns because, in the 5th century, there are indications that Western Europe was visited by several outbreaks or epidemics of plague. A port, even a river-port, in contact with ships from continental Europe, would be among the first to succumb to a 'pestilentia quae fere in toto orbe diffusa est' (Hydatius, c.443) and, as Wacher says, 'what better reason could we have for Saxons shunning towns if infected corpses were lying unburied in them?'

The Saxons gave Reading its name, but exactly in what form is not clear: the Old English name *Read* is derived from the colour, red, and 'Readingas' are the people of *Read(a)*. It is not to be supposed that the people were actually red themselves, so we must assume a patriarchal *Reada*. In Domesday Book it is *Reddinges*.

Its situation on the Thames with access, through the Kennet, to the hinterland of Berkshire probably ensured that, when the practice of commercial trading did begin to revive, it was in an excellent position to benefit from it. The foundation, in 1121 by the King himself, Henry I, of a Cluniac abbey for 100 monks, no doubt set the seal on the town's success.

The Abbey of Cluny in Burgundy in the early twelfth century had benefited immensely from a line of abbots renowned not only for their strength in authority but also for their longevity. Two only of them, for example, had covered the entire eleventh century. They had established Cluny as a model of the Rule of St Benedict and as a result monasteries all over western Europe wanted to be reformed in the Cluniac model. The abbot only stipulated that, if he consented to send a body of monks to reform an abbey, it should lose its independence; he would appoint a prior and all the monks, taking a vow of obedience to the abbot, would become in effect Cluniac monks, although still living in their own monastery. The advantage of this surrender of all rights to the authority of the Abbot of Cluny was that not only did they then share the very high repute of Cluny, but also its immunity from interference by either lay lords or secular bishops: Cluny would protect all its children. Henry I therefore, by founding a monastery and bestowing it on the Abbot of Cluny showed that he had every intention of creating a thorough-going Benedictine house, and none of interfering with its government or appointments for his own ends. The new abbey was colonised from Lewes, an established Cluniac house.

The remaining buildings of the abbey, which was comprehensively dismantled at the Dissolution, are scanty, but their scale gives a fair impression of the proportions of the abbey. There is a gatehouse, originally of the late thirteenth century but heavily restored by Scott in 1869, but more importantly at the end of Forbury Street alongside the wall of the County Goal, there is the only surviving masonry from the original structure: a part of the abbey church, the Chapter house, the Treasury, and the east wall of the Cloister. These thick flint-and-rubble walls are so massive that with a little imagination it is possible to picture the colossal grandeur of the whole. There is a model, based on the known foundations, of the abbey in the town's museum, which helps the process. The King, Henry I, was buried in the church somewhere.

Its numbers declined as the years passed: in 1305 there were 65 monks, in 1445 only 35, but the last abbot, Hugh Faringdon, did not give in to Henry VIII's visitors without a determined struggle, and like anyone else who stood in the way of that king, suffered for it. He refused to render an account of the abbey's revenues and treasures, was attainted of high treason, along with two of his monks, and in November 1539 they were all three hanged, drawn and quartered in Reading.

These poor remnants are almost the only survivors of Reading's mediaeval past, save for the parish church of St Laurence. It stands at the top of the Market Place and was originally just outside the abbey gates ('ante portas'). Although, as in the case of the majority of parish churches in Berkshire and everywhere else in England, there had been a church building of some sort on the site since the arrival of Christianity among the Anglo-Saxons, the present church dates from a period some 60 or 70 years after the abbey had been founded: there are signs in the south-east wall of the nave, and bits of a doorway re-set in the north aisle, of the twelfth-century structure, but extensive rebuilding took place in the early thirteenth century and again in the Perpendicular style of the fifteenth century. There are several brasses and a monument to a pioneer in the science of mathematics, John Blagrave, author of *The Mathematical Jewel*: he died in 1611. There is no old stained glass in the church, since it was all blasted out by near-miss bombs in the course of air-raids in the 1939-1945 war.

On the north side of the church there is a passage, a small garden, and a range of flint buildings partly of the fifteenth century; it belonged to the Hospitium of St John the Baptist, the customary lodging place for travellers and pilgrims at the gates of any monastic establishment, but the surviving part, of 1486, was actually added when the Hospitium was converted into a school.

At the far end of Forbury Gardens (in the middle of which is a large mound heaped up for defence purposes in the Civil War) on the site of one of the chapels of the abbey church, there is a Roman Catholic church appropriately in a Norman or Romanesque style, by the architect Pugin, in 1837-1840.

Like Abingdon, Reading's principal income depended on the cloth-trade by the time the abbey was dissolved, so that later in the century Leland could write that the town 'standith by clothing'. The father of Archbishop William Laud, who was born in Reading, was a clothier; the merchants built the kind of houses beloved of their kind, examples of which can be seen in many towns in southern England which also 'stood by clothing', and in the early eighteenth century Defoe could still describe it as 'very large, wealthy, handsomely built'. But the cloth-trade declined, and the corn-trade, via the all-important Kennet and Avon Canal, grew, and during the nineteenth century most of the town was pulled down and rebuilt. The famous biscuit factories were established, a new Corn Exchange, hospital, Town Hall and even Gaol were built. The Town Hall, or Municipal Buildings, in Blagrave Street north of St Laurence Church, were built in 1872-1875 and extended a few years later, in red and blue brick with all the Gothic eccentricity of the period. Newbury has a smaller version, complete with tower and clock. This *schloss* of Reading houses the public library, an art gallery, and a very good museum. The most important exhibits in the museum are those found at the site of Calleva Atrebatum, the capital of Roman Atrebatic Berkshire: we have seen how the whole area functioned in relation to Calleva by the radial road system from it to all quarters. The museum has beside models and reconstructions of what the houses, temples, baths and forum looked like (based on the foundations and assembled debris), a huge collection of fascinatingly mundane objects of everyday life there, many of which have hardly changed in shape or design to the present day; the whole presentation gives an impression of a level of civilisation, even to approach which the savage Germanic tribes who destroyed it needed more than a thousand years of development.

There are also in the museum some more implements and debris from the Mesolithic settlement at Thatcham, some Saxon ornaments, pottery and weapons, and a range of relics of the abbey, including a copy of the song 'Sumer is icumen in' by one of its monks.

Modern Reading, sprouting mighty office blocks, new industries and vast housing estates, is growing: the vital functions of river and canal have been supplanted first by the railway and now by the closely adjacent motorway connecting London with the West Country.

Caversham constitutes the only enclave of land belonging to Berkshire on the north side of the Thames. It sprawls out on rising ground from the river-level to the 'heights', offering little of real interest to the traveller except the parish church of St Peter which has traces of its Norman origin but was extensively rebuilt in 1878, and Queen Anne's School. The housing, principally, is from the nineteenth century on, and unless one happens to live there it does not grip the attention.

There is a stretch of Oxfordshire to cover before regaining south-of-the-river Berkshire, achieved by the long bridges across several branches of the river and then the humped brick bridge at Sonning. The houses of this very attractive village are grouped closely around a network of streets and passages, and include a number of timber-framed cottages (some painted white with blackened timber, uncharacteristic of Berkshire) and an inn, the Bull of the same construction, and some graceful brick houses of the late seventeenth and eighteenth centuries. The Dower House, in Pearson Street, looks William and Mary period; the Robert Palmer Cottages, dated 1850, are almshouses in mock Tudor.

The Bishop of Salisbury once held the manor of Sonning, and had a substantial palace there. The only remnant of it still standing is a high brick wall on the south side of the churchyard, but the site behind the wall was excavated in 1916 and the foundations were found of a hall and gatehouse of the fifteenth century, and the solar wing of an earlier manor-house. The wall is of Tudor date, and on the far side of its high arch now is a small extension of the churchyard and an agreeably untamed wilderness. The church is large and mostly Victorian, although earlier parts still exist. Some of the window tracery was certainly unknown in the middle ages!

A hill rises behind Sonning, and from it there is a wide prospect of the plain formed by the river's great meander, the land within which constitutes this part of Berkshire. After some new housing at Charvil the road crosses two converging branches of the Loddon, which joins the Thames about a mile away, below Shiplake. Donald Maxwell, in *A Pilgrimage of the Thames,* gives a Scotsman's advice to fellow-countrymen on how, if they are rowing up-river, to avoid paying the lock-fees at Shiplake. If, he says, they are genuine Scotsmen, they will not be put off by Pope's error in describing

The Loddon slow, with verdant alders crown'd,

since although it is certainly lined with alders it is equally certainly not slow, as they will discover when they have rowed up it for half a mile; but if they do this they will find another backwater which joins the Loddon on their right and if they row up that they will re-join the Thames at St Patrick's Bridge: they will have circumvented the necessity of passing through Shiplake Lock and saved the money for the fees. To support the appropriateness of this scheme Maxwell points out that the parish church of Sonning is St Andrew's.

The road to Henley sticks closely to the river bank and runs through Wargrave, not far below the mouth of the Loddon. The narrow streets have some remaining timbered cottages and two or three good Georgian houses, like Wargrave House on the corner of the High Street, and the Bull Hotel opposite. The church, away from the street across a wide green, was burnt down in 1914, only the brick tower of 1635 remaining, and is therefore rebuilt.

There begins at Wargrave (whose name has nothing to do with military cemeteries but means 'grove by the weirs') a range of low chalk hills which run across the northern part of the meander, an outcrop of the high Chilterns on the Oxfordshire side. The road cuts into the hills, high above the river. Around and among them in the grounds, now a golf-course, of Park Place, are some curious architectural and archaeological objects imported by General Conway who bought the house and 900 acres in 1752. They include the stones of Conway's Bridge, which the road uses, a collection of sarsens and other stones from, apparently, 14 different counties, some obelisks, a tunnel-vaulted Grotto, and a Druidic Temple which had been found in Jersey and given to the General in 1787. Some of these curiosities can be seen in between the trees and the golf-flags, but Park Place itself is hidden, which is not so important because it is not Conway's house but a replacement of 1870.

The riverside here is lined with summerhouses and boathouses all the way to Henley, the river itself busy with pleasure-boats. There does not seem to have been much pleasure about the first boat race between Oxford and Cambridge Universities, from Hambledon Lock to Henley Bridge in 1829: half-way through the boats collided, so they started again. As James Vincent says, '. . . for 2¼ miles up stream, rowed at high pressure, once and a half on the same evening, to say nothing of paddling twice to the starting point, in primitive eight-oars with keels, without outriggers, and on fixed seats, must have made it a struggle fully as trying as any of those that followed it.' Ten years later, in 1839, the first Henley Regatta was held: Henley itself is of course in Oxfordshire, but the Berkshire bank must claim its full share of these time-honoured and elegant proceedings.

Up the hill from Henley Bridge a footpath up a steep bank obviates the cruel necessity of following the busy A423 any further, cuts through the hill-top woods and emerges on a quiet lane to Remenham. It might be another world: the ear-splitting noise of the traffic on the hill is gone, its place taken by rural calm, and to the north is an idyllic scene of the tree-filled valley, flashes here and there of the silver river, the wood-rimmed hills of Oxfordshire (and, in fact, here of Buckinghamshire too) forming a green background wall: again, Berkshire's gift of tranquillity, a stone's throw from its vital arteries.

The parish of Remenham is extensive: Park Place, south of the Henley road, is within it, but the parish church is away in the far northern part of it, down by the river. It was restored in 1870, in flint, but looks appropriate, with a Norman-style apse. A lane clings to the lower hillsides above the river plain here, and gives a view of an island in the river where there is a little classical temple, a circlet of columns surmounted by a little green cupola. It belongs to Fawley Court, on the other side of the river opposite Remenham church, and was built as a 'folly' in 1771. Aston, still within Remenham parish, is a hamlet with an inn called the 'Flower Pot' and a working pottery, perhaps to justify it.

It is theoretically possible to go from Aston to Frogmill Farm by footpath, past a splendidly maintained Georgian house called Culham Court with grassy terraces and topiary down to the river, but the path keeps getting mixed up with farm tracks: in practice the project may well end in an illicit stroll along the farm road. Frogmill Farm has some chequered stone and flint work in its barn and adjacent buildings, which look eighteenth-century: from the nearby riverside cottages all the way to Hurley the riverside is lined with massed holiday caravans.

At Hurley William I, the Conqueror, founded at some date before 1087 a Benedictine monastery, which later became, as a Priory, a cell of Westminster Abbey. The first to be seen of its surviving buildings, if approached from the west, is the barn and circular dovecote added in the fourteenth century. On the far side of a quiet green, close to the river, are the other remnants: the refectory range, now part of a private house, in stone and flint, and on the south side of its courtyard the nave of the Priory church, which is the parish church. It is long and narrow, with Norman windows and doorways, but was extended twice in subsequent centuries. On the left of the sanctuary is a fresh-painted monument to John Lovelace and his wife of Ladye Place. The Priory had been dedicated to the Virgin Mary: after its dissolution the parts extending southward from the church were demolished and a private house named after it took its place. John Lovelace, who died in 1558 was its builder. His grandson Richard was, according to Fuller, 'a gentleman of mettle; and in the reign of Queen Elizabeth, making use of letters of mark, had the success to light on a large remnant of the King of Spain's cloth of silver, I mean his West Indian fleet; wherewith he and his posterity are warmer to this day'.

In 1599 Lovelace was one of the worthies knighted by the Earl of Essex in Dublin, an action which infuriated the Queen because it exceeded his authority. Essex's knights were nevertheless permitted to keep their honours, and in 1627 Lovelace was ennobled, as Baron Lovelace of Hurley, by Charles I. The family was remotely related to the Lovelaces of Bethersden, in Kent, which produced the Royalist poet Richard Lovelace.

The family became extinct about 1736, but the mansion, which was rebuilt by the 'warm' Sir Richard in 1600, was still standing in Dugdale's time. None of it remains above ground now. Beneath its foundations there has been discovered the vaulted undercroft of what was probably the Priory's infirmary, but the site is now occupied by some modern houses.

From Hurley to Bisham a footpath goes through Temple Park, some woods and a queer and eerie tunnel, and comes out at Temple Mills. The recurrence of the name Temple recalls that the manor was held by the Order of Knights Templar, whose original function was to defend the Latin Kingdom of Jerusalem from Muslim incursions, but that having been found impossible, continued to hold great wealth and became bankers until they were suppressed without clear reason and with great brutality by King Philip IV of France, 'le Roi de fer'. At Bisham they had a preceptory, and after their suppression there was founded in 1337 an Augustinian priory, which exactly 200 years later was re-founded as a Benedictine Abbey. Considering the way the Tudor wind was blowing, at gale force against religious houses because, partly, of their links with the Catholic Church of Rome, but also because Thomas Cromwell had pointed out to the King that they owned a great quantity of desirable wealth, the establishment of a new abbey seems more gallant than advisable, as they said about Lord Falkland's suicidal ride at First Newbury. It was duly dissolved three years later.

Probably the only place from which one can see the Abbey properly is the other side of the river: it certainly is not possible from the Berkshire side. Approaching from the direction of Temple Mills the only part visible is a collection of barns and outhouses, mostly now inhabited; a service road runs around it, but it is defended by a fierce black dog. This is a pity, because the house contains a good deal of thirteenth-century work of the Templars' time, and some of the Augustinian canons', as well as the later structures which converted it into a mansion for the Hoby family to whom it was granted after the Dissolution.

The road politely side-steps away from the Abbey and its guardian dog, and runs past a huge, bleak brick building, like a power station, being built behind the Abbey. It is, apparently, a sports hall and hostel, for the Sports Council. Town Farm, on the east of the road through Bisham, is a more agreeable sight, a big timber-framed house with a hipped tiled roof, whose four storeys of lateral framework give it something of the look of a house of cards. Terraced Georgian cottages line the road, and right at the end of the village its parish church stands so near the river bank that one can sit on a bench close to the walls and feed the ducks.

The tower of All Saints, Bisham, although patched and repaired, is still essentially late Norman, 1170-1180. The rest of the church was restored in 1849, but the chapel devoted to the Hoby family is still more or less sixteenth-century, with heraldic glass in its east window. The monuments are in excellent condition: Lady Margaret Hoby's is worth a long journey to see. It is of alabaster, a plinth, an obelisk and on each corner a swan, beautifully sculpted. According to Pevsner it is 'one of the most original monuments of the age'.

Who were the Hobys, why were they granted the manor, and why are they so commemorated in the church? They were diplomats, they were honoured for service to their monarch, and they were given memorials because they paid for them.

Sir Philip Hoby was a son of William Hoby of Leominster and obscurity; his enthusiasm for Henry VIII's church reform brought him to the King's notice, and he became a diplomat for him in Spain and Portugal. At that time membership of the Diplomatic Corps did not preclude armed service, and for his conduct at the siege of Boulogne in 1544 the King knighted him. The manor of Bisham was granted him by the young Edward VI in 1552, and being a skilled diplomatist he did not let his Protestantism prevent him from serving Queen Mary. He died in his house at Blackfriars, London, in 1558 and was buried at Bisham. He had no son so left his estate to his half-brother, Thomas, who was also a diplomat, travelled a good deal and spoke several languages, an accomplishment he shared with his wife, Elizabeth, a daughter of Sir Anthony Cooke. Cooke had been brought into Court by Queen Catherine Parr as tutor to young Prince Edward, and his four daughters were reckoned the most intelligent and gifted of all the ladies of their time; the marriages of two of them had a profound influence on the future course of events, since one became the wife of Sir William Cecil and the other, of Sir Nicholas Bacon, both of whose sons played central roles in Jacobean politics. Elizabeth's husband, Sir Thomas Hoby, died when only 36, so she re-married, in 1574, John, Lord Russell, a member of another Tudor family who rose to the aristocracy of later years.

The son of Elizabeth and Sir Thomas, Edward, with the advantage of having Lord Burghley (William Cecil) as an uncle, swiftly rose to prominence at Court, and went on a number of diplomatic missions. He was knighted the day after he married the daughter of the Queen's Champion, Lord Hunsdon: she was Margaret, the lady of the swans. Sir Edward entertained both Queen Elizabeth and James I at Bisham Abbey.

It is not far from Bisham to Marlow Bridge, where the pleasures of the riverside scene can be viewed at leisure from the sunlit terraces of the Compleat Angler inn. The steep hills of Quarry Wood rise sharply behind the main road A404 which crosses the river by another bridge downstream from the older one, and the woods screen a spread of housing around Cookham and Cookham Dean which fills much of the country north of Maidenhead.

Maidenhead itself is not a beautiful town, but obviously efforts have been made, by rebuilding sections of the town centre, creating pedestrian precincts and obliging the traffic to avoid it, to give it a character of its own: more time is probably necessary fairly to judge it. According to Dugdale the town owes its growth to the building of a new bridge in 1297 and the re-routing of the great western road across it. The present bridge was built in the late eighteenth century, and the railway bridge, whose arches at 128 feet each were said to be the biggest-ever span in brick, was one of Brunel's to carry his Great Western Railway. As mediaeval Maidenhead may have developed because of the important route through it, so did modern Maidenhead because of the railway.

The complexity of motorways and main roads south of Maidenhead have rendered impossible the usual Berkshire facility for

22 Church Street, Windsor

Drury
House
RESTAURANT
Fine Old
Furniture
Nell Gwynne
NELL
A.D. 1640

ER
NO DOGS
NO CYCLES

peace and quiet away from them, but Bray, squeezed in between river, railway and roads, still manages to preserve an element of rural charm. Although its High Street serves as a B road and therefore supports much traffic, the houses have not changed greatly: there are timber-framed cottages, brick houses of the eighteenth century like Chantry House by the churchyard, the Crown inn, disguised by two projecting brick wings but centrally a fourteenth-century timbered hall-house, and the Jesus Hospital, founded in 1627 by bequest from William Goddard, who had died in 1609: his statue stands in a niche in the brick gatehouse. There is now a modern quadrangle of apartment blocks, in another side-road, showing pleasing variety in conformation and colour of bricks, with balconies which the residents have decorated with baskets of flowers and creepers.

But best of all there is the Lych Cottage, under which one passes to enter the churchyard; it is a timber-framed cottage, tiled and in-filled with brick, and on the churchyard side has a little wooden gallery on the first floor. It was built in the fifteenth century. On the other side of the church, in the churchyard, there is a little flint Chantry Chapel, which in the seventeenth century became a school. On the outside of the south-facing wall there is a mysterious relief sculpture of a horse: it looks as if it might have a Norman origin.

The church is big, and has its original Perpendicular tower, but is otherwise all 1859 restoration. The tower, the Lych Cottage and the Chantry Chapel, however, along with at least some of the High Street cottages, would all have been there when Simon Symonds alias Alleyn was the vicar.

The well-known song, 'The Vicar of Bray', although apt enough in sentiment, has transferred the Vicar to the vicissitudes of religious doctrine in the reigns of Charles II, James II, William III, Anne and George I. The historical person, according to Thomas Fuller, who described his career in his *Church History,* belonged to another age. Here is his account.

> 'When King Henry VIII shook off the papal supremacy, the vicar of Bray preached in the most zealous manner against the innovations and encroachments made by the court of Rome; and when the Five Articles were published, he vindicated idolatry with

23 The Round Tower, Windsor Castle

all the strength of prostituted logic. In the reign of Edward VI when the protestant religion was established by act of Parliament, the vicar renounced all his former principles, and became a strenuous advocate for the Reformation. On the accession of Queen Mary, he again vindicated the doctrines of the church of Rome, and became a zealous papist, inveighing with great acrimony against all those worthy persons who abhorred the Romish religion. He enjoyed his benefice until the reformed religion was established in the reign of Queen Elizabeth, when he once more changed with the times, and enjoyed his vicarage until his death, which happened in the 41st year of her reign. This man's name was Symon Symonds. So insensible was he of everything, that bore the name of moral honesty, that instead of being in the least affected by it, his constant answer was, "I will live and die vicar of Bray."'

Another corner of old Berkshire now encircled by the maze of motorways is Ockwells Manor House, the best example of a timber-framed fifteenth-century house in England. It was built by Sir John Norris between 1446 and 1466; the manor of Ockholt in the parish of Bray (a huge parish: no wonder the unspeakable Symonds was so bent on keeping the living) had been granted to his ancestor Richard de Norreys because he had been cook to Queen Eleanor, wife of Henry III. This was in 1267; the Norrises came originally from Speke in Lancashire, and it was to a son of Sir Henry Norris of Speke that the Ockholt property came more than a hundred years after the grant. His great-grandson John made a career at Court, as any ambitious person needed to do: he was first usher to the chamber under Henry VI, then squire of the body, master of the wardrobe, and sheriff of Oxfordshire and Berkshire; he seems to have had something of the 'Vicar of Bray' spirit himself, because he also became squire of the body to Edward IV. Evidently he did not enjoy the finished Ockwells for long, because he died in 1467 and was buried in the church of Bray. It was one of his sons, William, who also changed sides and was rewarded by Henry VII with the manor still known as Hampstead Norris.

Another odd little corner is the island in the Thames half a mile below Bray Lock called Monkey Island. It can be reached by a lane going south from Bray over the M4, but the track to the island is private, belonging to a hotel; the hotel is in a fishing lodge built for the 3rd Duke of Marlborough in about 1744. The painter Clermont decorated its interior with pictures of monkeys indulging in all the ducal sports, fishing, shooting and hunting.

TEN

Royal Berkshire

In 1957, Queen Elizabeth II approved of the continued use by the county authorities of the description 'Royal County of Berkshire'. She confirmed, regally, a practice which had existed, unofficially, for many years, because of the associations of the county with the royal residence at Windsor Castle. I have therefore used the title for this last chapter-heading.

In time, perhaps, Wokingham's houses will extend along the railway-side to join Reading's and Bracknell's: there is not far to go. Two huge forest areas, Windsor and Bramshill (once one), prevent a future eastern Berkshire from becoming one big housing estate, engulfing the remaining agricultural areas.

Wokingham so far still retains the essential quality of a country town: precariously, perhaps, because of the ever-growing extensions, but the town centre has not been demolished piece-meal and replaced by the duplicated shop-fronts that recur in every shopping street around London. Approaching from the railway station, there is first Shute End, a road with a grassy bank and a row of several centuries' contribution to domestic architecture, ending in a timber-framed house called, probably correctly, Tudor House. It faces the aptly named Broad Street, which also has some good houses, and leads to the junction at the centre of the town where, in an island, the Town Hall stands. Considering that all new building is usually contrasted unfavourably with the old, the recent row of shops that curves round the corner from this central point, in dark red brick and an element of unobtrusive quality, must have caused far less controversy when new than the Town Hall, in 1860. Even now its orange and dark brick and its combination of Gothic, Byzantine and French château effects are startling. The best building in the town is the Lucas Hospital (which is actually out of town, south of the railway-line where it branches off to Bracknell). Here is Dugdale's description of its foundation:

> 'At Luckley or Lockerley Green, in this parish, is an hospital for 16 pensioners, founded by Henry Lucas, who died in 1663. The pensioners are allowed £14 per annum, and are chosen alternately by 16 parishes in Berkshire, and the same number in Surrey. A chaplain has apartments in the hospital, and salary of £70 per annum. The original bequest is said to have amounted to £7,000, of which nearly £2,500 was laid out in the erection of the necessary buildings, and the residue invested in the purchase of lands in Bedfordshire. The drapers' company of London act as trustees for this charity.'

Here again is the compensating factor, often encountered, of one of the wealthy merchants of the period when the weight of political power in England shifted from the land-owning aristocracy to the up-and-coming commercial gentry, all desirous of becoming in their turn land-owning aristocracy. The new ruling class frequently wished to show that they too could be generous patrons, benefactors, philanthropists, and to do the thing properly a man bequeathing the really substantial amount of £7,000 to found a charity had to ensure that his money bought investments to provide it with an income and that it was administered by reputable trustees. The Lucas Hospital was well built in 1665.

The church of Wokingham is built (mainly in 1864-1866) in sandstone, but the tower and clerestory are dark brown stone, a substance known as conglomerate; it is a kind of natural concrete, because the gravelly subsoil of the Bagshot Heath area has been 'cemented' by ironstone. The church stands in Wiltshire Road, a name which commemorates the surprising fact that this part of Wokingham actually was an enclave or insulated section of Wiltshire. Considering that the nearest border with Wiltshire is in the region of Hungerford, on the other side of the county, this anomaly might seem to take a bit of explaining. It is a survival of the manorial system of the middle ages, existed in Dugdale's time and slumbered on until comparatively recently. A great landowner might hold manors in a number of different parts of the country as we have seen in the various cases of manors belonging to the Abbot of Reading, or Abingdon, or to the Prince of Wales, or to John of Gaunt, or to the King, or any of the dukes and earls. F. W. Maitland, writing of the time of Domesday Book, says that 'proprietary rights have already been making sport of arrangements which in our eyes should be fixed by public law. Earls, sheriffs and others have enjoyed a marvellous power of taking a tract of land out of one district and placing it, or "making it lie" in another district'. Even after the passage of centuries these detached 'parcels' of land continued to pay rents and dues to their manorial lord, usually now some county council, until the inevitable tidy-minded civil servant noticed it, reminded his minister, and all was ironed out.

Despite the houses and motorways, the country north of Wokingham is arable and pastoral and enjoys the usual Berkshire attribute of freedom from motor-traffic; there are farms, cattle and corn, trees and hedges, and one might even see a mobile blacksmith in action at a roadside field-gate.

Binfield is a remarkably widespread place which appears to have been a kind of eighteenth-century garden suburb, judging from the number of gentleman's seats within the parish. Binfield Lodge, Park House and Manor House are all Georgian, and so is the house the poet Alexander Pope was supposed to have inhabited: since the Popes left it in 1716 Dugdale's reference to the site of Pope's house seems more likely.

The Pope family moved out to Binfield from London in about 1700, Pope senior having acquired wealth from his trade of linen-drapery. Alexander was then 12 and had suffered a serious illness which distorted his figure: it was brought about, they said, by 'perpetual application', because he was precocious and was for ever reading and writing. He became acquainted with a local worthy, Sir William Trumbull who had once been a Secretary of State, and with the playwright Wycherley, who introduced him to his literary circle in London. While at Binfield Pope wrote and published his

'Pastorals', 'Essay on Criticism' and 'The Rape of the Lock'. His poem about the Loddon and another on Windsor Forest appeared while he was within physical reach of both. He was extremely fond of the countryside, and the name Popeswood, south of Binfield, probably commemorates a part of a wood where on a tree were once inscribed the words HERE POPE SUNG.

The oldest house in Binfield is probably Binfield Place, on the road west, part of which is a Jacobean manor-house in brick and tile, with gables. Binfield Park, now a hospital, is probably the biggest, and therefore corresponds with 'the most conspicuous', once the seat of a gentleman with the resounding name of Onesiphorus Elliot, Esquire. The church, also in dark brown conglomerate, is partly Victorian and fractionally mediaeval (the tower is Perpendicular and so is the south aisle) and contains a palimpsest brass: on one side an early fifteenth-century abbot, the other side re-used for Richard Turner and his wife in 1558. There is also a marvellous iron stand for the pulpit hour-glass, in wrought iron with animals, oaks and grapes among the decorations.

There are quiet country lanes to be found to grace the way to Warfield, which is a normal Berkshire village, on a hill, within sight of the massed roofs and towers of Bracknell and beyond. It is a small hamlet clustered around its church and manor-house on the ancient pattern. The church, the third in this district in the pebbly conglomerate, has been built up over the years from the simple late Norman nave which is now the north aisle; a chapel, a new nave, and a tower were added in succeeding church-building periods, and finally the chancel was restored, rather horribly, by Street in the 1870s. The four-light screen between the north aisle and the chapel, with the rood-loft still above, are rare indeed.

Two timber-framed cottages bordering the churchyard complete the picture, both brick in-filled and tiled, from the early seventeenth century; one is the Parish Room, a single-storey hall, and the other is called St Michael's Cottage (the church's dedication).

The country, still heavily afforested, is now also heavily populated, from Winkfield Row to Chavey Down, a kind of forest suburb with bungalows and suburban types of houses in the woodland. On the road down to Ascot a mass of thick tall trees encloses Ascot Priory, a

Victorian Gothic house built to house the Society of the Holy Trinity, which was founded in Devonport in 1848 by a friend of Dr Edward Bouverie-Pusey called Priscilla Lydia Sellon.

North of the noise-filled road from Bracknell lie the massed houses; south of it, a woodland lake called Englemere Pond; east of it a crossroads and the famous race-course. The whole of the north side of the road that runs south of the course is filled with the mighty brick buildings, stables, stands, gates, parking areas, officials' offices, usual offices, and the great royal gate marked ER II for Royal Ascot occasions.

The Royal Ascot Hotel, just north of the crossroads, was for a brief period between the wars transformed, out of the customary contemporary crude dullness which characterised so many provincial hotels in England, into a vision of future possibilities by the imagination and personality of John Fothergill.

For nine years he had run the Spreadeagle at Thame, giving it his own culinary expertise, bringing to a country inn delicacies unknown to rough English palates, and creating a reputation which brought to his inn gourmets, conversationalists, critics and wits from Oxford, London, and farther afield. But pioneers in anything, like Jethro Tull, are seldom permitted to flourish because the majority of their paying contemporaries are too dull-witted to understand them or share their vision. Fothergill sold the Spreadeagle at a loss, and was persuaded by a brewery to make himself into a company and take on the big, unlovely Royal Ascot Hotel, which was really only a paying proposition during Ascot week, when it was crammed to the brink.

Fothergill decided that what he could do at Thame he could repeat, on a wider canvas, at Ascot: he would change the two dining-rooms and make them beautiful, he would paint the courtyard loose-boxes with a rainbow perspective of colour, he would decorate the ballroom with 'a series of graded shades of rose or fuchsia beginning at the end of the room and tapering to a vanishing point where they meet in the centre of the end wall'. He would put the hotel on the map so that people would come to it for the sake of its food, wine and accommodation, and not just as a convenience to be endured for five days in the year. 'An hotel', Fothergill wrote, 'has to grow up round the owner and take his shape, just as his own boots and clothes do. It is that permanently-maintained-tailor-made and pressed condition of the clothes of a swagger hotel that proves the lack of legs, feet and body of humanity underneath. So Inns can have souls as well as bodies.'

But although he had attracted the beginnings of a clientèle, he had also attracted the beginning and end of criticism and had spent heavily. His accounts did not balance, he had no profit to show his directors and they were incapable of looking further forward to a day when his innovative potential could be fully realised; they voted for liquidation and Fothergill was ruined. Nowadays, like Tull's machinery and methods 50 years after him, the imaginative ideas and good taste of Fothergill are taken for granted, if not fully implemented, by every good restaurant and hotel in the land.

Ascot racing, as was mentioned in connection with his stables at East Ilsley, was put on its feet by the Duke of Cumberland, although it had been originated in about 1711 by Queen Anne. The Duke lived at Cumberland Lodge and sometimes at Cranbourne Lodge, on the western edge of the forest, because he had been appointed warden of Cranbourne Chase, as that tract is called. With his deputy ranger, Thomas Sandby, he improved the park with plantations of Scotch firs and cedars, and put in motion the creation of Virginia Water, half of which only is now in Berkshire because the boundary runs across it from Sunningdale, past Cumberland Lodge and out to the Thames-side road by Beaumont College, which was built as a house in 1790 and turned into a college for Jesuits in 1861, so that it has a part-Georgian and part-Gothic look.

At the riverside the A30 road meets the A308: to turn right is to enter Surrey and the precincts of one of the most famous sites in England. Runnymede is no longer an island, just a flat meadow with the road running through, and cars and people all over it, and it is impossible to be certain of quite where King John agreed to compromise, by a 'social contract', with his version of the T.U.C.

In order to avoid the worst excesses of 'new' Old Windsor, it is possible to take a footpath from Runnymede along the riverbank to the church, which is near the river (the modern houses are on either side of the main road), if not quite so near it as Bisham. It has been quite well restored, by Scott, but is basically Early English, with small lancet windows, a triplet of them in the east wall of the chancel.

Old Windsor was the original holder of the name, which is a very unusual one: it appears as 'Windlesora' in about 1050 and as 'Windlesores' in Domesday Book, and seems to derive from the words 'windan', to wind, and 'ora', bank, combining apparently to mean, 'a river-bank with winding gear'. What sort of winding-gear, and what was wound up on it?

Whatever the goods or objects landed at this highly mechanized landing-place, they might have been connected with a palace which the Anglo-Saxon kings, with reasonable certainty, possessed there. But there is also evidence of Roman occupation, so perhaps the machinery, if that is what existed, could more plausibly be credited to them. Evidence either way appears to be entirely lacking. William the Conqueror, looking for defensible positions on the great river, found one in the mound near the riverbank in the manor of Clewer, north of Old Windsor, so after some horse-trading of manors with the monks of Westminster Abbey, to whom his predecessor King Edward had granted it, he built the first castle on it, of wood. Old Windsor continued to exist, and a settlement developed around the walls of the castle. By 1242 we may read of both 'Nova et Vetus Wyndelesor' as the castle's town assumed greater importance.

The Home Park of Windsor Castle occupies the whole promontory in a meander of the river between Eton and Albert Bridge, with the castle itself opposite the former place; the town has developed westward of the Park, in the former parish of Clewer. Part of the grounds were also in the parish of Orton, which has disappeared.

That the castle's mound is a natural hump of chalk and not yet another artificial motte, raised perhaps as an Iron Age hill-fort (most of those were on natural hills anyway), is no longer in dispute. There is still argument, however, concerning the first stone walls: some say the round tower was begun by Henry II, others that the early foundations are those of 1075, which supposes that King William built something more substantial than a wooden keep and stockade on his knoll by the river. Whatever the facts of the masonry, the two huge baileys are typical of early Norman castle design, and there existed by 1122 a structure magnificent enough to be appropriate to a royal marriage: Henry I's, for the second time. Henry II, an enthusiastic castle builder, built a shell keep 34 feet high, rebuilt the curtain-wall, with projecting towers, round the baileys, and raised apartments for himself in the Upper Ward, whose vaults lie beneath the present royal apartments.

John's confrontation with his magnates and their rebellion after he had sent to the Pope to annul the Great Charter brought the only serious siege the castle has known. John had plenty of support in the country, partly from the loyal elder statesmen like William the Marshal and Earl Ranulph of Chester, partly from loyal commoners like 'Willikins of the Weald' who led a Robin Hood-like band of guerrillas against the French allies of the rebels in Sussex and Kent, and partly from his own mercenary captains, who owed their lives and careers to the King and whose positions were among the most hotly resented grievances expressed in the Charter: the King had enriched these 'foreigners' with lands confiscated from rightful tenants without trial. One of the captains, Engelard de Cigogné, held Windsor against the rebels throughout the summer of 1216; by September some of the rebel leaders had been killed, some had changed sides, and the opportunity to counter-attack was taken by John, who marched from the Cotswolds down the Thames valley, drew off the besiegers of Windsor and headed for the eastern counties, from which he never returned.

The damages of the siege were repaired by John's son, Henry III, and three of his towers remain intact; it was Edward III, who was born in the castle and was therefore known when a child as Edward of Windsor, who created a new tradition for the castle when he created his Order of the Garter and glorified the hitherto virtually ignored patron Saint George in an attempt to kindle his subjects' enthusiasm for supporting him against the French king. He built a chapel and housing for canons, choristers and other officials of the Order, and increased his own quarters in the Upper Ward.

In 1389, the year in which Edward's grandson Richard II began the long process of winning back the initiative against his 'council', Geoffrey Chaucer, poet and civil servant, was appointed Clerk of the King's Works, in the course of which he had to superintend repairs to the Chapel of St George. Unfortunately for Chaucer there is no way of knowing how good a builder he was (there are certain other ways by which he is better remembered) because some 90 years later Edward IV caused the old chapel to be demolished and a new one erected.

The work began in 1475, and the result is the acme of mediaeval architectural achievement, the end of the progression towards the art of building in stone gracefully, giving maximum height, width, light from the greatest possible window-space; the most satisfying way to make a ceiling; and above all the sense of perfection, that the art form could go no further than this. The work occupied skilled craftsmen for 50 years, the fan-vaulting being completed in 1528. The Knights of the Garter continued to use it as their own chapel, and their carved wooden stalls occupy the dramatic centre of the chapel: each knight hangs his banner over his stall, but the arms of his predecessors in the stall, on little painted shields, climb the dark wooden back. All the knights have been and are (with a few exceptions) men of the highest rank both in position and in character, so that a list of their names reads like a catalogue of chapter-headings for an English history.

Kings and Queens of England lie buried in the chapel, some with chapels of their own, some ornate, some simple. Edward IV had his own tomb built, with an accompanying coffin to accommodate his wife, Elizabeth Woodville, one of the most insidious 'femmes fatales' in history. Here is one of Dugdale's stories, about these tombs:

> 'On 13 March 1789, the workmen who were employed in repairing the chapel, perceived a small aperture in the side of the vault where Edward was interred; and on the interior part being laid open, the skeleton of the monarch was found enclosed in a leaden and wooden coffin, the latter measuring 6 feet 3 inches in length . . . Near the bones of the king was another coffin, supposed to have contained the body of Elizabeth Woodville, but it was entirely empty.'

So despite her ambitious schemes, neither she nor her sons found a place among the royal skeletons of England.

Henry VIII built the main entrance-gate, named after him, very early in his reign (while he still had money to spend) and it is one of the last of its kind to be built with military intentions. Neither he nor his children contributed anything else to the castle, and it was not until the end of the seventeenth century that it received any more royal attention, from Charles II, who demanded an improvement in the comforts of the accommodation. A new range of apartments arose in the Upper Ward.

The Hanoverians seldom used Windsor, and it fell into disrepair; George IV, however, had a taste for splendour lacking in his forefathers. Evidence of it still remains, in the Pavilion at Brighton, Buckingham Palace, and here at Windsor: near the end of his life he and the architect Wyatt (who changed his name to Wyatville) planned and executed the wholesale repairs, additions and improvements that stand today and give the whole castle the look of having been built from scratch in the 1820s. The rebuilding cost a million pounds, and George his last possible chance of popularity, since the country was suffering from a long post-war slump at the time, and poverty was widespread.

Queen Victoria used the castle, as can be seen by nearly all the grandiose furnishings of the State Apartments, some of which typify Victorian design at its ugliest. The crowning disaster is the mausoleum, attached to the east of St George's Chapel to house Prince Albert's and her own tombs: as a contrast to the chapel, it has to be seen to be believed. Victoria did, however, initiate a regular use of the castle by reigning monarchs, complete with a full social programme while in residence, and her successors have maintained it.

There is much to see in Windsor; so many people from all over the world come to visit the castle that watching them can constitute a whole day's fascinating employment, but over the heads of the crowd there is still so much of the place to admire: the timber-framed, brick-nogged Horseshoe Cloisters, for example, built with the chapel to accommodate the chapel clergy (and incidentally the finest example extant of the Berkshire vernacular style); the King's Beasts, high on the walls of the chapel, or the view from the topmost battlements ofthe Round Tower. There are paintings in the State Apartments which are worth a visit for their sake alone: George IV commissioned the artist Lawrence to paint many of them. There is also the famous doll's house which still attracts long lines of people waiting to see it. Armour, weapons, relics, furniture, porcelain, paintings: all these things separately give pleasure and interest;

together and in Windsor Castle they give more, a sense of belonging not only to the royal personages who have used and handled them, but also to the ordinary folk who come in their thousands to look at and admire them.

The things that have just been described are material and tangible things, but Windsor has more than them, it has above all a concentration of memories, of events and the personalities of the men and women who acted their parts in them. Despite the crush of people any day at Windsor Castle, the Babel of their voices, the flourishing of their cameras, the good-humoured patter of the guides, it is not hard to imagine (passing through the dark gateways and stone passages, watching the sunlight glowing through the bright colours of the chapel windows, standing on some high battlemented tower and seeing the whole great edifice, an accumulation of work of many men in many centuries, laid out below), time slipping away, the events re-enacted, the personalities speaking.

It is Whit Sunday, 1095, and King William Rufus is in session with all his councillors: all, that is, except the Earl of Northumbria, who refuses to attend. The King with his councillors plans a campaign against the Earl. At Christmas, when Rufus once more holds court at Windsor, Earl Robert is there, sure enough, but not sharing the King's table: he is in one of the dungeons. The furious Rufus had gone to Northumbria, besieged the Earl's castle at Bamburgh and erected a fortress of his own before it, called 'Malvoisin': one night the Earl tried to escape to Tynemouth, but the garrison of the new castle saw him and took him. Rufus returned, had the Earl brought before Bamburgh and informed his wife and nephew that both of his eyes would be put out unless they would surrender the castle. The castle doors were opened, the Earl's eyes were spared and, if perhaps reluctantly, he was there at Windsor when the King held his Christmas court.

Christmas again, 31 years later: William Rufus's brother is holding court, Henry I, and this is a most important occasion. His only legitimate son has been drowned, and despite his re-marriage (here, in the castle) there are still no male heirs. King David of the Scots is present, and so are all the greatest men in England, ecclesiastic and lay. They are to be witnesses to the King's proclamation, that after his death, England and Normandy shall pass into the possession of his daughter Maud, widow of the late Emperor of Germany; (a murmur of dismay can be heard among the rough greybearded barons: a woman to rule? No good could come of that); and furthermore, the King is telling them that forthwith the Empress shall go to Normandy, accompanied by her half-brother Robert, Earl of Gloucester, and she shall marry Geoffrey Martel, son of the Count of Anjou. More than a murmur is heard now for this scheme is hateful to all: is not Anjou the ancient enemy of Normandy, and if Maud is to be Queen, will not the Count of Anjou be King, and what vengeance will he demand from old enemies, by seizure of lands, distraint, attainders, imprisonment? The seeds of discontent are sown, to bear fruit within ten years when the Normans proclaim their choice for the crown, Stephen of Boulogne.

King John is at Windsor, in the spring of 1205; he has planned a brief holiday for himself from the hard itinerant life of a mediaeval monarch, intends to indulge in his favourite occupation, hunting, in the great forest which stretches for many miles either side of the Thames; and for his relaxation he has asked his faithful steward Reginald of Cornhill to send him two tuns of wine, and 'a history of England in French'.

Henry III is there, in the perilous days when the arrogant Earl Simon of Leicester is insisting that he knows best how to govern the kingdom: he has had the temerity to summon three knights from every shire to meet in an assembly at St Albans; the King summons three more from every shire to meet him at Windsor, and they tell him on whom he can rely against the powerful de Montfort. As a result he summons 150 tenants-in-chief to bring their knights to his side. A month later at Kingston the baronial leaders make their peace with him, leaving Earl Simon without support: 'It is the English way', he observes in disgust, 'to lead a man into a tight corner, and then let him down'. He sails for France, and for a space the King rules again.

The King's son, Prince Edward, now king himself in 1276, never forgave Earl Simon until he had beaten and killed him at Evesham in battle. But his family had revived his anger: a son, Guy de Montfort had murdered Edward's cousin, and now a daughter, Eleanor, was on her way from France to marry Llywelyn, Prince of Wales, without his overlord the king of England's permission. The King's ships intercept the bridal convoy off the Scilly Isles, and Eleanor de Montfort is brought to Windsor Castle, where she stays, fretting and unhappy, for two years, until the King has taught the presumptuous Welsh prince a lesson.

All the pageantry and heraldry of the creation of the Order of the Garter is here at Windsor, a new Round Table with a new Arthur, King Edward III, athletic, warlike, chivalrous (and greedy and rather unintelligent, but never mind); the castle is renewed in a material and spiritual sense, with a new chapel. In another age and an entirely different atmosphere, with the long war against France irrevocably lost and the country torn by the agonies of civil war, there is another great rebuilding by another Edward, and the beginning of the most beautiful chapel the age had seen. The son of an enemy finishes it and builds the last great castle gateway of the middle ages, his mind full of the glories of past chivalric achievements, of war with the old enemy, France, of great deeds of physical valour, never dreaming of the humiliation of 20 years' marriage without a living son, or of the cataclysmic upheavals in state and religion in his efforts to get one. His daughter, the great Elizabeth, comes and goes, holds brilliant court in the Castle, flirts with Robert Dudley, always willing to walk among her subjects, talk with them and be their Queen.

Another queen sits in the apartments built in the Upper Ward by her uncle, waiting for news of her army's fortunes. Its commander the Duke of Marlborough had marched it away from the old battlefields in the Netherlands to save Vienna from the French. Already, as Colonel Parkes rides into Windsor, through the gateway and up to the Round Tower, the town knows the news and the cheering can be heard even from within the castle; Parkes, admitted to the Queen's presence, kneels and gives her a scrappy bit of paper, an innkeeper's bill. He has already shown it to Duchess Sarah, in London. The Queen reads:

> I have not time to say more but to beg you will give my duty to the Queen, and let her know her army has had a Glorious Victory. Monsieur Tallard and two other Generals are in my Coach and I am following the rest . . . .'

Marlborough's victory at Blenheim has made the plain, plump woman one of the greatest sovereigns in Europe.

An old man is living his life away in the neglected castle, a pathetic figure in a purple dressing-gown, with a wild white beard, totally blind, totally deaf, totally mad: he talks incessantly, to the trees in the Park, to his harpsichord as he plays it, to himself most of all, talking to men and women long since dead about events long since over; he is free now from the crushing strain of duty, from the intolerable necessity to 'be a king, George', when he had not the mental ability to bear such responsibility. He had been a king, of the great maritime nation which had triumphed over the arms of France in India, in Canada and at sea; then he had led that nation into a disastrous war with its own colonies and had lost it, and them. Now, his mind gone, his health improved because of the absence of strain, he seems to his disreputable eldest son to be likely to live for ever.

But he dies at last, the son reigns, and raises at Windsor the finest set of State Apartments it has ever yet boasted; he hardly has time to occupy them.

Victoria is at Windsor: at first, (Greville, 1838):

'. . . Windsor is totally unlike any other place. There is none of the sociability which makes the agreeableness of an English country house; there is no room in which the guests assemble, sit, lounge and talk as they please and when they please . . . When the meal is over everybody disperses, and nothing but another meal reunites the company, so that, in fact, there is no society whatever, little trouble, little etiquette, but very little resource or amusement.'

By the end (1898), in the kitchens at Windsor:

'were prepared every day the meals for all the lower servants, as well as the breakfasts and ten- or twelve-course luncheons and dinners served to the Queen, the Royal Family, their guests, the lords and ladies-in-waiting who were in residence. I had expected to see one Chef in white overall and magnificent chef's toque, but there were eighteen of these men besides M. Ménager the Royal

Chef, eight of them with their own tables in various parts of the kitchen . . .'*

War with Germany in 1914, and the King has abandoned Saxe-Coburg-Gotha in favour of Windsor: the name of the castle has become the name of the dynasty.

The town of New Windsor, now just Windsor, has grown up as the castle has grown up. Edward IV's enormous building programme brought houses to the town: the Market Cross House, a little plastered timbered house, leaning at a perilous angle, is probably from this time. Charles II initiated a similar aggrandisement of the castle and touched off another spate in the town, from which came some of the houses in Church Street and the Town Hall itself. It was designed by Sir Thomas Fitch, but he died before it was finished, and the work was completed, in about 1690, by Sir Christopher Wren, whose plans worried the town councillors because they thought the building would be unsafe, and ought to be supported on columns. Wren knew perfectly well that his structure would stand for as long as it was wanted, but even his reputation would not convince them: there must be columns. Very well, columns should be built: but Wren had the last laugh. He built their columns, but made sure that they did not actually touch the ceiling.

George IV's massive rebuilding brought the nineteenth-century's first contribution to Windsor town, and Victoria and the Great Western Railway added still more. There are plenty of modern supplements, particularly in the spread of the housing estates, the twentieth century's speciality, throughout the parish of Clewer to Clewer Green and Oakley Green, but central Windsor is still dominated by work of the nineteenth century.

Since 1974 the Royal County of Berkshire has extended beyond Windsor, across the river to include Eton and Slough. I have disregarded the new boundaries in order to describe the Vale of White Horse, which had belonged to Berkshire for all time until 1974, but by the same logic I regret that I wish to leave these newly acquired territories to some chronicler of Buckinghamshire. Eton can speak for itself, in any case, and who am I to echo Sir John Betjeman's sentiments on poor old Slough?

* Gabriel Tschumi, *Royal Chef,* 1954

Index